1980

Creator and
Heroic Deed

Solzhenitsyn:
Creator
&
Heroic Deed

LEONID RZHEVSKY

Translated by Sonja Miller

The University of Alabama Press
University, Alabama

Library of Congress Cataloging in Publication Data

Rzhevskiĭ, Leonid Denisovich, 1905–
    Creator & heroic deed.

    Translation of Tvorets i podvig.
    Includes bibliographical references and index.
    1. Solzhenitsyn, Aleksandr Isaevich, 1918–   —Crit-
icism and interpretation.   I. Title.
PG3488.04Z8713   891.7′3′44   77-13643
ISBN 0-8173-7900-2

Translated by Sonja Miller from the Russian,
Tvorets i Podvig, Copyright © 1972 by Possev-Verlag,
Frankfurt am Main, Federal Republic of Germany

Contents

891.73
869...

89716

Foreword

The title of this book conveys its inner impulse—praise to courage and talent united in verbal creation.

The author, nevertheless, renounces any deep sociological interpretation of the theme "heroic deed," in spite of the bravery and pungency of the recently published *Gulag Archipelago*. That which attracts the author, above all, is the craftsmanship of Solzhenitsyn the artist.

This is not to say that no one doubts this craftsmanship. Such people have always existed—"There is the salt of the earth and there are faults of the earth." (Andrey Voznesensky, "Antiworlds.") More important, the exposure of craftsmanship is the basic path for the understanding of art. Hence the textual orientation, the abundance of quotations, and the attention to areas where the verbal creation is presented in its greatest degree of strength and beauty. Hence (in the second and last essays) the attempt to determine what is new in the language and poetics of Solzhenitsyn's prose.

There is another "renunciation"—a renunciation of comparisons with contemporary Western literature. Solzhenitsyn is, to a great degree, immune from its influences, perhaps because of the artificial "curtains," in addition to prison and exile. But more likely it is because of the organic *počvennost'* of his muse. Examples of Western influence encountered in foreign analyses usually draw together elements that have "ontological," external similarities, but are different causally. For example, the symbolism of Camus's *The Plague* ("there exist those people who can get accustomed to conditions of the plague, and those who would want to escape from those conditions"); this could, of course be extended to the East, but it would only be an analogy. It would hardly help us to understand Solzhenitsyn's craftsmanship.

The author of these essays of course does not consider them in any way exhaustive. The style of the narrative phrase, the structure of dialogue, time in the novels of Solzhenitsyn are among the many hardly yet touched themes!

The author all the same hopes that this book will find its place on the shelves of criticism, present and future, of the works of Alexander Solzhenitsyn.

This book was translated from the published Russian edition. The author wishes to thank David Frolich and—especially—Sonja Miller, who brought this translation to its present form.

L. R.

Creator and Heroic Deed

1

Creator and
Heroic Deed

A creator always reveals himself in his creations and often against his will.
— N. Karamzin

One's ability to perform a heroic deed, a deed beyond the strength of an ordinary individual, partly arises from one's will and partly seems to be inborn.
— A. Solzhenitsyn

1

A certain conversation was overheard near the lecture hall.
"What's the lecture about?"
"The works of Solzhenitsyn."
"That's the wrong idea."
"Why is it wrong?"
"It should be 'The Heroic Deed of Solzhenitsyn.'"
"You think so?"
"Everyone thinks so. Everywhere there is fear and baseness, and he alone ventures forth. Declaring conscience, truth, and steadfastness for every people—isn't that a heroic deed?"

It seems to be true. "Conscience, truth, and steadfastness" are declarations of Solzhenitsyn's creative work and his heroic deeds simultaneously. His artistic self-consciousness lies in the tradition of Pushkin's "Prophet."[1] To the Fourth Writers' Congress of the USSR Solzhenitsyn wrote, "my literary task I will fulfill under all conditions, and from the grave even more successfully and indisputably than when alive."
We are reminded of Dostoevsky—the way he, thoughtfully and "inwardly turning," would read Pushkin's "Set the hearts of men on fire with your word" (Glagolom žgi serdca ljudej); the way he had loved one of Ogarev's verses ending with the wish:

Čtob vyšla mne po vole roka
I žizn', i skorb', i smert' proroka.

(That I should have through the will of fate the life, the grief, and the death of a prophet.)

We have before us the age-old tradition of Russian literature, that which Thomas Mann at one time called "sacred" for its deep humanism, a humanism embodied in the creative word of the writer, a ruler of men's minds.

A Scandinavian critic, Per Egil Hegge, writes in reference to Solzhenitsyn's novel *August 1914:*

> Solzhenitsyn would like his works to become well known, because according to the Russian literary tradition he considers a writer's expression necessary for the people, an idea which is shared even by the majority of loyal Soviet authors. This firm belief in the mission of literature is today foreign to us Scandinavians, for us it is old-fashioned and in any case belongs to a century that has passed.

Suppose that the contemporary Scandinavian reader is no longer able to imagine a new Ibsen or Strindberg as a ruler of his mind, that faith in the mission of literature seems too old-fashioned to him, then what about the feelings of people outside Scandinavia? Is it possible that the works of Joyce and Sartre, Hemingway and T. S. Eliot, do not move the reader, challenge his mind, pose any questions?

Bearing in mind the essence not only of Russian literature but of verbal creation in general, Chekhov, an objective artist who is so close to our contemporary life, wrote in a letter to Suvorin: "writers whom we call eternal or just good, writers who intoxicate us, have one general and extremely important characteristic in common: they are going somewhere and they lead you there, and you feel not just intellectually but with all your being that they have a certain purpose, like the ghost of Hamlet's father who had a reason for appearing and stimulating our imaginations."

And from another letter to Suvorin: "For he who sincerely believes that the highest and most distant goals are of as little need for a man as for a cow, all that is left to do is to eat, drink, sleep, and when these bore him, to run around banging his head against the wall."

We can, without being polemical, make another simple explanatory point concerning Hegge's article: Solzhenitsyn is not continuing but reviving the humanistic traditions of Russian literature extinguished in the postrevolutionary period. It is necessary to speak about this in more detail.

Among the short stories by Solzhenitsyn there is one entitled "The Ashes of the Poet" (Prax Poeta). It concerns the grave of a poet, Yakov Polonsky, who instructed that he be buried in the cemetery at the monastery overlooking the river Oka. Later the same cemetery happens to be in the vicinity of a Stalinist prison camp.

The camp overseer explains to visitors:

> There was a monastery here. The second greatest in the world. The greatest, they say, was in Rome and the third in Moscow. When the children's colony was located there, the children didn't know what the place was, so they messed up the walls and broke all the icons. Then a collective farm bought both churches for forty thousand rubles—wanted the bricks for a six-stalled cowshed.... A crypt was found under the church. The bishop had been buried there. He himself was just a skeleton but his robe had been preserved. A couple of us tried to rip the robe in two but we couldn't tear it. (6:53)[3]

Is it coincidental or symbolic that in 1871 Yakov Polonsky himself wrote the following poem on the writer's mission in Russia for Elena Andreevna Shtakenschneider's album? (She was the daughter of an architect whose home was the meeting place of free-thinkers in those days.)

Pisatel'—esli tol'ko on
Volna, a okean—Rossija,
Ne možet byt' ne vozmuščen,
Kogda vozmuščena stixija.

Pisatel', esli tol'ko on
Est' nerv velikogo naroda,
Ne možet byt' ne poražen,
Kogda poražena svoboda.

(The writer, if he is a wave and the ocean is Russia, cannot be still when the elements are astir. A writer, if he is the very nerve of a great people, cannot be undisturbed when freedom is disturbed.)

Later, in the wake of the first Russian revolution, government cruelty evoked an indignant response on more than one occasion. First published in translation in the West in 1906, Lev Tolstoy's story "The Divine and the Human" (Božeskoe i čelovečeskoe) deals with the execution of a certain student, Svetlogub, who is unjustly accused of terrorist activity. Two years later Tolstoy's "I Cannot Remain Silent" was published. This work inspired Leonid Andreyev's *The Seven Who Were Hanged,* which appeared shortly thereafter. "I feel that at present I don't have an actual voice, and I want to scream, 'Don't hang them, you scoundrel,'" Andreyev writes to Gorky. Russian literature during the period between the two revolutions enjoyed a status of independence. The October 1917 Revolution destroyed that status. In the post-revolutionary twenties the very concept of an independent creative literature was subjugated. "The twenties," we read in *The History of Soviet Russian Literature,* "was a period of intense struggle against anti-Soviet trends in order to establish a basic artistic course—the assertion of the method of Socialist Realism as the fundamental method of Soviet literature."[4]

Pressured by this "assertion" even the most brilliant voices of protest grew silent—"Art has always been independent of life, and its colors never reflected the color of the flag above the fortress," wrote Victor Shklovsky.

Genuine writers, declared Yevgeny Zamyatin, are always "madmen, heretics, dreamers, rebels." Zamyatin indicated his concern for the fate of creative literature in a sentence that was to become a catchword: "Russian literature has only one future—its past."[5]

Boris Pasternak believed that the effects of the elimination of creative freedom were already felt by the end of the twenties. In his *Autobiographical Sketch* he writes: "In the last years of Mayakovsky's life, when there was no more poetry, neither his nor anyone else's, when Yesenin had hung himself, *when, frankly speaking, literature had ceased to exist....*"[6] The italicized text was deleted from the text by the editors of the *Novyi Mir* (New World).

Established by the early thirties, "socialist realism" was above all a secret formula that prohibited critical realism, a tradition known for its impatience with injustice and its love of mankind. An enormous list of themes and revelations involving the most diverse aspects of human life as well as the expression of the human soul became taboo for Soviet writers of the thirties and forties. Violating this taboo meant opposing the only allowable ideology in the USSR.

Preserving the taboo was guaranteed by a terror that invoked a fear so great that no one dared to write a new story of *The Seven Who Were Hanged* or to cry, even if only in private correspondence, "Don't hang him, you scoundrel." That those executed could probably be counted in the hundreds of thousands was unimportant.

The writer's missionary self-consciousness with respect to his country and to the truth died away. The "Prophet" became silent. The unified conscience of the Soviet Writers' Union kept silent as its members one by one were taken away to be executed or exiled. "We discovered after the Party's 20th Congress that more than six hundred writers, who were guilty of absolutely nothing, were obediently handed over by the Union to their prison camp fate," Solzhenitsyn wrote to the Fourth Writers' Congress.

With his characteristic turn of poetic expression and double meanings, Boris Pasternak notes the relationship of silence and protest in 1931:

Naprasno v dni velikogo soveta,
Gde vyšsej strasti otdany mesta,
Ostavlena vakansija poeta:
Ona opasna, esli ne pusta.

(Wrongfully, in the days of the great Soviet where preference is given to the higher passions, the poet's place is left vacant—it is dangerous, if not empty.)

And some thirty years later one of Solzhenitsyn's characters states this somewhat differently: "a great writer is, so to speak, the country's second government. And this is why no regime has ever loved its great writers, only its minor ones" (4:503).

The great writer Alexander Solzhenitsyn is also not loved by his country's government because he has resurrected the lost tradition of the "Prophet," because, as a foreign reviewer of his works writes, he alone "has returned our literature to its unusual love of truth and to the eternal Russian ethical themes."[7]

2

The writer's task "concerns secrets of the human heart and conscience, the confrontation of life and death . . . and those laws of humanity as a whole, germinated in the forgotten depths of the millennium, will
cease to exist only when the sun is extinguished," said Solzhenitsyn at
the meeting of the Secretariat of the Writers' Union (6: 53). The theme
of conscience, this sleeping beauty so to speak of postrevolutionary
literature, resounds abundantly and polyphonically in his creations.

Ivan Denisovich possesses a real conscience and an inner purity.
Even when in great need "he did not give nor take bribes and didn't
even pick up that bit of knowledge in camp."

"Listen, do you know what I sometimes think?" the inmate Nemov
tells his interlocutress in the play *The Deer and Shalashovka,* "Maybe
our hide is not really the most valuable thing we own?"

> *Ljuba:* (very attentively) Then what?
> *Nemov:* In camp, it is somehow awkward to say . . . Maybe when all is
> said and done . . . conscience is.
> *Ljuba:* (looks intently) You think so? . . . (5: 84)

Alex and Philip, characters in another play by Solzhenitsyn, *The
Candle in the Wind,* argue about the limits of conscience.

> *Alex:* . . . Life is a one time thing. But there is something else that we
> have once and we don't get a second chance.
>
> . . .
>
> *Philip:* Eh, brother, say something a bit stronger. Conscience? To live by
> it in the twentieth century is too nonmaterialistic. . . . Conscience is a
> feeling left to choice.

". . . strangely enough, the lower I sink into this cruel and inhuman
world, the more keenly I respond to the few persons in it who appeal to
my conscience," states Nerzhin, the autobiographical hero of *The First
Circle.* And the voice of conscience determines his relationship to
Simochka, who is in love with him, although he relinquishes her love
after the unexpected visit with his wife, probably his last:

"She [his wife] won't wait for me? Let her not wait. Let me die not needed by anybody in the Krasnojarsk taiga. But if you know at death that you haven't been a scoundrel, that's at least some satisfaction" (4: 716).

Solzhenitsyn depicts the awakening of conscience even when it should be lulled in the soul of man. Ruska Doronin, one of the youngest inmates of the *sharashka* in the same novel, becomes a double agent hardly out of bravado; he betrays the informers, who were recruited by the MGB, to his fellow prisoners.

The awakening of conscience in the brilliant young diplomat Innokenty Volodin is the pivot of the plot in *The First Circle*. Not only life but also "conscience is given to us only once"—this conclusion by Volodin reiterates Alex's statement cited above from *The Candle in the Wind*. It becomes the title of the fifty-fifth chapter of the novel.

In a conversation about writers, resembling an interrogation, Galakhov, the writer laureate, asks Volodin, his brother-in-law, "That means that they remind you of our conscience?" "Reading your journals, I would say—Not always," Volodin answers.

"I know of only two misfortunes in life—remorse and sickness," said Lev Tolstoy.

However, Solzhenitsyn regards remorse as the realization of a blessing, like "the last remaining virtue of a criminal" (Voltaire), which leads to repentance and thus to the cleansing of the soul.

The past torments Rubin, probably the most talented of the intellectuals in the *sharashka* (*The First Circle*); he has remained a Communist even in prison. At one time he had supported collectivization—violence against the uncooperative, death and hunger to a village.

"I ruined many women. Left them with children. They cried . . . ," Yefrem Podduyev confesses at the threshold of death, suffering from cancer of the tongue.

Conscience and justice are conjugate concepts. "What is the most valuable thing in the world? It seems to be the realization that you have not taken part in injustice," repeats Volodin following the voice of conscience. According to Tolstoy conscience is "the memory of society, comprehended through separate individuals." In other words, it is a kind of standard regulating society as well as private life.

In Solzhenitsyn's "Answer to Three Students" the definition is refined in the following way: Justice "is not relative as is conscience. It is conscience, not the personal kind but that of all humanity at once. The individual who clearly hears the voice of his own conscience is the same individual who generally hears the voice of justice" (5: 269).

Solzhenitsyn's most journalistic story, *For the Good of the Cause,* is devoted to the breach of justice as a collective feeling.

Arkady Belinkov, the critic, entitled his article on Solzhenitsyn in *Time* (27 September 1968) "The Writer as Russia's Conscience." Solzhenitsyn is at least the conscience of modern Russian literature.

As Venyamin Kaverin stated at a discussion of *Cancer Ward* at the Moscow Writers' Organization on 16 November 1966—characteristic of Solzhenitsyn are "two invaluable traits, inner freedom and a powerful striving for truth" (6: 159).

This was repeated by Y. Karyakin at the same discussion. "In Dostoevsky's notes," he recalled, "the following statement is found: What if Tolstoy had lied, if Goncharov had lied? What kind of immorality would there have been if these individuals had lied? But for Solzhenitsyn it is an inconceivable proposition. He does not lie."

Proponents of truthfulness in the literary art could not help but take into consideration the fact that in the thirties and forties the very idea of truth underwent a specific reinterpretation directed, above all, at overcoming the traditions of critical realism. In exchange there emerged a required orientation for writers, namely, that their works promoted "the communist education of the masses." This orientation became known as "the method of socialist realism."

A great émigré poet commented aptly on this change:

> Ved' dlja togo že socialističeskij
> I suščestvuet realizm,
> Čtoby nikto ne mog realističeski
> Izobražat' socializm.

> (Why, it is for this reason that socialist realism exists: so that no one can describe socialism realistically.)

Anna Karavaeva was one of those writers who dethroned critical realism together with the traditional interpretation of truth. In her article "About the Most Cherished Man" (Joseph Stalin) published in volume 12 of *Novyj Mir,* 1949, she wrote:

Critical realism, which began as a method of reflection upon the gloomy pre-revolutionary reality, bequeathed the tradition of depicting suffering. . . . Writers most often found life's truth through a negative precept: that which is bad is truth. . . . Where is truth? Is it to bring forth in a narrative a negligent kolkhoz worker or delinquent, or is it to place the main threads of action and the interpretation of events into the hands of a character who will encourage individuals to go forward with the people [that is, with the party]? Of course actual truth is always a second choice.

Such a conclusion needs little comment. The merging of "truthfulness" and "party principle" was a constant critical trend of the times. "A work which is neither truthful nor party-oriented cannot be a work of art," wrote the *Literaturnaja Gazeta*.

The previously polarized ideas of truth and falsehood were drawn together and fused by a kind of artificial clouding.

I. Vinnichenko, one of the participants in the above-mentioned discussion of Solzhenitsyn's works, had just such a fusion in mind when he cited the expression "to lie the truth." Solzhenitsyn "is a writer who is essentially not able 'to lie the truth,' " he said.

In *The First Circle* Solzhenitsyn gives a vivid illustration of a writer's method that is based on the ability "to lie the truth." One of the inmates of the *sharashka,* engineer Khorobrov, weary of the inactivity of a Saturday evening (that same December 1949 when Karavaeva's article on "truth" appeared) looks in vain for a book to read.

The books on the pile were fiction, but to read them made Khorobrov sick to his stomach. One was the new best-seller, *Far from Us,* which was now being widely read on the outside. But after reading some of it Khorobrov felt a wave of nausea. The book was a meat pie without the meat, an egg with its contents sucked out, a dead bird stuffed. It talked about construction which had been carried out by zeks [prisoners], about camps—but nowhere were the camps named, nor did it say that the workers were zeks, that they were given prison rations and jailed in cells; instead they were transformed into members of the Komsomol, well dressed, well shod, and very enthusiastic. Here the experienced reader would sense that the author himself had known, seen and touched the truth, that he might even have been an administrative officer in a camp, but that he was lying with cold, glassy eyes. (3: 124)

The actual title of the book alluded to is *Far from Moscow*. Its author, Vasily Azhaev, received the Stalin Prize of the First Order. He was actually a kind of administrative overseer at one of the Stalinist camps; he depicted the prisoners' forced labor on a pipeline across the taiga in winter as a massive enthusiasm for socialist construction.[8]

In *The First Circle* Solzhenitsyn analyzes the essence of the creative process paralyzed by the writer's anticipation of censorship. As a result his best conceptions and perceptions writhe and perish in the embryo stage. The writer-laureate Galakhov is oppressed by the fact that "his plays, his stories and his novel have died before his eyes even before the author has reached the age of thirty seven.... there is glory but no immortality."

There are many similarities and correspondences that permit one to assume that the prototype of Galakhov is Konstantin Simonov, a diversely talented writer whose work is significantly degraded by the "method" of the party line. In the collection *Den' poezii* (The Day of Poetry) of 1956—the first and last collection of the literary "thaw"— we find the following epigram on Simonov:

> Vseizvesten, mnogogranen,
> Zaspektaklen, zaekranen,
> I vesom,
>   i mnogosvjazen
> I pri vsem—
>   odnoobrazen.

(Known to all, many-faceted, on the stage, on the screen, weighty, and influential, and before all—monotonous.)

The narration of Galakhov's story by Solzhenitsyn reveals the nature of such monotony: "much of the truth could not be written." Perhaps in the future, but meanwhile "One should write that quarter, eighth, sixteenth, damn it, that thirty-second fraction of the truth—whatever possible. Something was better than nothing" (4: 505–506).

But what happens to the writer's inspiration on this thirty-second fraction of the truth?

> Each time he started a great new work, he would get all fired up, swear to himself and to his friends that this time he would not make concessions

to anyone, that this time he would write a genuine work. For the first few pages he was enthusiastic. But he very quickly noted that he was not writing alone, that before him loomed the image of the person for whom he was writing and with whose eyes he was involuntarily rereading every new paragraph. That person was neither the reader,—brother, friend, peer—nor even critics in general, but always the celebrated principal critic, Zhabov.

... And so paragraph after paragraph, striving to anticipate Zhabov's arguments and to adapt himself to them, Galakhov would quickly modify statements and the book would faintheartedly roll out and fall into place.

By the time he was halfway through, Galakhov would notice that his book had changed—once again it wasn't working out. (4: 506–507)

An invaluable characteristic of Solzhenitsyn's "internal freedom" noted by V. Kaverin is embodied not only in an apology for conscience, justice, truth, and other worthy aspects of the human spirit but in the steadfastness of this spirit in the face of any kind of enslavement. The proclamation of good is inevitably accompanied by the negation of evil, which sometimes disturbs certain critics. Is not accusation a form of politics? However, great artists are entitled to affirm and negate through "the literary form," especially when that form has been well polished. Pushkin's attitude toward the problems of freedom and constraint are found not in his early, youthful works but in "The Bronze Horseman."

The literary manifestations of steadfastness and accusation in Solzhenitsyn are rich and varied. We will discuss these in more detail in the following essays evaluating individual works. However, we can mention several examples here:

(*a*) "Try to be cooler—this gives another's sorrow a background upon which it can be shown in bolder relief," Chekhov wrote to L. A. Avilov in reference to her literary attempts. "The more objective, the stronger the impression."

The grief of victims of terror is often described by Solzhenitsyn in this Chekhovian epic manner; the tragic fate of several *sharashka* prisoners (engineer Potapov, for example), the Kadmins (*Cancer Ward*), and many others are presented without a trace of authorial "pressure." The scenes and episodes of Solzhenitsyn's first narrative (*One Day in the Life of Ivan Denisovich*) are so visual and so clear precisely because of the cool, simple, and faithful narrative technique. For example, the environment at the front: "This is what happened. In February of '42 their army was completely surrounded on the northwestern front. No food was parachuted to them and there weren't any planes for it. It got so bad that they scraped the hooves off dead horses, let the horn seep in water and ate it. They had no ammunition. So the Germans caught them in the forest a few at a time and took them prisoner" (1: 52).

(*b*) The steadfastness of the authorial "I" finds direct expression, needless to say, in the author's evaluations and commentaries, which sometimes take the form of digressions—heated emotional castigations of Stalinism, its past crimes and its present repercussions. "It was so excessive, so crude, so beyond everything that only an elephant's ear could hear the lies," reflects the authorial Nerzhin on the purges and trials of the thirties (*The First Circle*). And further: "Can it be that the people didn't hear? Russian writers who could trace their genealogy from Pushkin and Tolstoy were oppressively heaping saccharine praise on the tyrant. Russian composers educated on Herzen street jostled one another to shove their obsequious compositions at his pedestal" (3: 285).

We note the author's same agitated castigation in an essay relevant to our times, "The Easter Procession:" "A religious procession without supplicators! A religious procession with caps, smoking cigarettes, transistors in breast pockets.... What is to become of these millions we have bred and reared? Where has the enlightened efforts and reassuring visions of great thinkers led us? What good can we expect of our future generations?" (5: 237).

(*c*) Steadfastness emerges in certain places in the very tone of narration—the author's irony and sarcasm embodied in several forms. For example, in the chapter "The Party Secretary" (*The First Circle*) Stepanov's duty is to maintain a high ideological level among the workers in a "special jail" and to guard them against the harmful influence of cosmopolitanism and servility toward the West. From party references received by Stepanov from the Obcom (the local Communist Party office) we learn the following about Stepanov: "social origin—farm hand, after the Revolution—a rural policeman, does not have a profession,... education—four grades of elementary school and two years of Party schooling,... on Party assignment since 1923, has never shown vacillation in the advancement of the Party line,... has never been abroad, knows no foreign languages, knows none of the national languages of the USSR, shell shocked, awarded the order of the 'Red Star' and the medal 'For Victory in the War of the Fatherland Against Germany.'"

The chapter ends with these lines: "It also put him [Stepanov] in a good mood to remember that the pink-eared baby pig he had bought yesterday had gladly eaten its mush both evening and morning without fuss. This gave promise that it could be fattened cheaply and easily" (4: 630).

(*d*) Satiric accents within the plot and such insertions as "The Traitor Prince" and "Buddha's Smile" will be discussed below.

(*e*) A distinct subtext (underlying or hidden textual meaning) of accusation and irreconcilability both in the language of characters, in their monologues, and in various expressive remarks. For example, the story of how the Brigade Leader Tjurin, son of a former kulak (a wealthy peasant) was driven from the army (1: 66–69); Kostoglotov's comments about his fiancee, who like himself found herself behind barbed wire ("Can you imagine what awaits a girl in a prison camp if she's good looking. If she's not raped in some hole in the ground on the way by anyone, they can always succeed in doing that in camp,—on the first evening some of the camp parasites—those damn overseeing dogs, or else the ones who give out the rations—set it up for her to be taken naked to the bathhouse so they can have a look at her on the way" (2: 492); and also some of the most ruthless condemnations of the epoch of fear and police obscurantism are found in Shulubin's monologues in *Cancer Ward*.

In the dialogues and discussions between several pairs of characters (Rubin and Sologdin, Kostoglotov and Rusanov, for example) the castigation of obligatory dogmatism and party control over thought and speech at times reaches great heights.

(*f*) The very characters of the narratives are the embodiments of accusation and protest. "How he would love to break through these thick skulls and demonstrate justice, even if it was tiny, miserable, but just the same—justice. Then at least he would have taken a stand to maintain his personal identity," we read about Kostoglotov (2: 580). Bobynin, as *sharashka* engineer, becomes unforgettable because of his steadfast attitude toward his jailers. "You need me and I don't need you.'' He tells the fearsome Abakumov. ''You took my freedom away long ago and you don't have the power to return it since you don't have it yourself'' (3: 118).

3

Rejection of evil is expressed by Solzhenitsyn in a powerful creative spectrum. Expressed so courageously! ''One's ability to perform a heroic deed, a deed beyond the strength of an ordinary individual, partly arises from one's will and partly seems to be inborn.'' These lines used as the epigraph for this chapter are found in *The First Circle* (4: 680).

The reader wishes to imagine as fully as possible the image of this heroic author, as it is manifested in his books; figuratively speaking, he has inscribed the creative and the spiritual essence of his art upon the banner of Russian literature, raised high above the world by him.

''A creator,'' wrote Karamzin, ''always reveals himself in his creations and often against his will. . . . You take up pen and want to be a writer: ask yourself when you are alone, without witnesses—honestly, what kind of person am I? For you want to write a portrait of your heart and soul.''

''In a work of art the most important element is the soul of the author,'' said Lev Tolstoy.

Alas, we lack the direct contact that might make clear the image of Solzhenitsyn, the artist. Very rarely does he give interviews. Incidentally, one of these, recorded by the Soviet journalist B. Bukhanov in the early days of Solzhenitsyn's fame, contains several interesting quotations. The author did not yet have to be cunning or to guard against openness. ''One month,'' we read at the beginning of the interview,[9] ''would be sufficient for this provincial teacher's name to be known all over Moscow and Vladivostok, all over Paris, in the wintercamps, in the Antarctic,'' and further, an indication of the author's personality: ''His reticence, his polite reserve, is simply staggering. He doesn't speak of the past and makes no prognosis about the future. In general he speaks little and only when necessary. Stubbornly, I would say fiercely, he insists upon his right not to say anything about his work. The path from writer to reader is only through his books; he repeated to me, time and time again. . . . He has a personal distaste for any sort of publicity.''

This ''staggering'' reserve and ''distaste'' not only for publicity but perhaps also for the interviewer himself, in whom a former prisoner might not feel a special trust, are not simply external or accidental traits. They are repeated in nearly all of Solzhenitsyn's main fictional characters whom we can consider more or less autobiographical, or, in other words, of a kindred spirit and aspiration with the author. The recent front-line soldier Rodion Nemov of the play *The Deer and Shalashovka,* Alex of the play *Candle in the Wind,* Nerzhin in *The First Circle,* and in *Cancer Ward* Kostoglotov, who "never allowed himself to smile at the jailers even if they smiled at him"—all are autobiographical.[10]

There are even deeper traits that unite all these heroes: all of them are at heart rebellious lovers of truth, defenders of justice, individuals with a strict measure of conscience toward themselves and their surroundings; all of them have endured years of prison camps; all, in one way or another, are undergoing a kind of catharsis, a reexamination of their former views of life, a rebirth to another, a higher, spirituality.

Here is Alex, the hero of the most "abstract" of Solzhenitsyn's works, *The Candle in the Wind.* He has served in "The Desert of Caledonia" nine years of his ten-year sentence—a mistake of the court. "Lost years!" "A curse on all jails!" he is told in the play.

> *Alex* (sighs): No, it's not that easy. There are moments when I say: God bless you, prison!" (5: 127)[11]

Gleb Nerzhin reflects that it was Sologdin who "first gave him the impetus to think that a person did not have to regard jail solely as a curse but also as a blessing" (3: 192). "Perhaps we shouldn't be sorry that we have served five years," he thinks, "they have a value of their own. Where else can you get to know people better than here? And to think about yourself?" (3: 353). And finally in the chapter "The Banquet Table," during the birthday party: "Friends," Nerzhin exclaims, "I swear to you that I will never forget the genuine majesty of the individual I have discovered in prison" (4: 448).

This again prompts us to recall Dostoevsky, who acknowledged that in penal servitude "I reexamined all of my past life . . . judged myself mercilessly, severely, and sometimes even blessed fate for granting me the solitude without which I could have made neither this judgment upon myself nor the strict reexamination of my past life."

Nerzhin's philosophy of *počvenničestvo,*[12] also the result of a self-reexamination, is by nature close to that of Dostoyevsky's, but it seems to be narrower, more personal, closer to the Tolstoyan quest for personal spiritual harmony. The chapter "Going to the People," the story of Spiridon whose outlook on life, according to Nerzhin, somehow coincides "with the Tolstoyan truth that in the world there are neither righteous nor guilty individuals"; the theme of *What Men Live By* (Čěm ljudi živy) and the theme of "moral socialism" in *Cancer Ward,* the theme of "the irrationality of history" in *August 1914*—yes, behind the author's own image that emerges from Solzhenitsyn's books, distinctly arises the ghost of Tolstoy.

It is in the Rousseauism of several autobiographical heroes: Nerzhin's aspiration toward plain living—"to rid himself entirely of the habits of intellectual politeness and flabbiness"; the repudiation of civilization's successes: "Did Plato have a storage battery? Did Mozart have two hundred and twenty volts? The heart reveals itself by candlelight, uncle," says Alex (*Candle in the Wind*).

The elaboration of several Tolstoyan motifs and concepts in Solzhenitsyn is not a repetition but a renewal of them on new, apologetic heights. They are inseparable from the conditions of free thought and free speech in Solzhenitsyn's homeland, conditions in which being "against the current" means being heroic. Many spiritual values, earlier irrefutable, stand in need of defense.

"Every moral is relative!" says one of Alex's adversaries.

"Damn the relativity of morals!" he answers. "You can justify any wrongdoing with the relativity of morals. To rape a girl is always bad in any society! and to beat up a child! and to throw a mother out of her home! and to spread slander! and to break a promise! and to violate a confidence!" (5: 184).

That which needs defending is, above all, the unworldly spirit with which Solzhenitsyn endows some of his characters; that sense of non-materialistic beauty, which finds expression in the chapter "The Church of St. John the Baptist" (*The First Circle*); that turning to heaven, to eternity, to some source of explanation, of insight into life, which breaks through many of the lines.

At this point it would be an injustice, perhaps a mistake, not to mention Pasternak's *Zhivago,* a novel-parable whose inner theme is a defense of the human soul and its right to turn idealistically toward higher sources of spiritual wealth.

Pasternak decoded the meaning of the parable in an interview by a Swedish critic in this way: "During the short period of time that we live in this world we have to understand our attitude toward existence, our place in the universe. Otherwise, life is meaningless. This, as I understand it, means a rejection of the nineteenth century materialistic world view, means a resurrection of our interior life, a resurrection of religion—not in the sense of religious church dogma but as an attitude toward the universe."[13]

Many of Solzhenitsyn's heroes could ascribe to this. Both writers make a personal apology for the talented and for those who search for the truth. Pasternak writes: "Every herd instinct is a refuge for the mediocre, whether it is loyalty to Soloviev, or to Kant, or to Marx. Only individuals seek truth, and they shun all those who do not love truth sufficiently."[14] Solzhenitsyn writes: "the Colossus of the Spirit is based not on their [people's] great number. Only brilliant individual personalities, like twinkling stars scattered through the dark sky of existence, carry within them a higher understanding" (4: 540–541).

The image of a flickering candle is for both writers the symbol of the human soul in need of care. It is fulfilled in Pasternak's poem "Winter Night" (Zimnjaja noč') contained in the last section of poetry in the novel.

Melo, melo po vsej zemle
Vo vse predely.
Sveča gorela na stole,
Sveča gorela. . . .

(It snowed and snowed the whole world over, from end to end. A candle burned on the table, a candle burned.)

This image is repeated in Lara's remark to Yuri Zhivago: "And you continue to flicker and give warmth, my brilliant little candle!"

Solzhenitsyn has written a play with the conventional Leonid Andreyev symbolism—*The Candle in the Wind.* Alda, the girl whom Alex loves, undergoes experimental "neurostabilization" designed to make her immune to the waves of life, to create a "granite spiritual health" within her.

"She is a little candle!" says Alex. "She is a quivering little candle in our terrible wind!" "Don't blow her out. Don't harm her."

And later he says: "How I would like to help pass the baton—the undulating candlelight of our soul—to it [the twenty-first century]. (5: 199–200).

So, for the reader of Solzhenitsyn's works the image of the author gradually takes shape.

In his preface to *The Works of Guy de Maupassant,* Lev Tolstoy wrote:

"In essence when we read or contemplate an artistic work our basic question is the following: 'Well, what kind of person are you, and how different are you from all the other people that I know, and what can you tell me that is new in regard to the question of how to look at our life?'"

Perhaps the answer to this question, summing up all that has been written above, is contained in two lines from Alexander Solzhenitsyn's letter to the Fourth Congress of Soviet Writers—a short formula for heroic action: "I do not block anyone from the path of truth; for its course I am ready to accept death."

2

The Resurrection
of Language

We must deal with the word honestly.

—N. Gogol

1

The writer's craft begins with his language.

Solzhenitsyn is undoubtedly an innovator in the field of language. His efforts to enliven the modern Russian language with the freshness and richness of popular speech, to soften the congealed bookishness, lifelessness, and platitudes in the literary language with living conversational elements, which are themselves based on the honesty and directness characteristic of common speech—these are his innovations.

But before presenting forms and examples of these innovations, it is important to note the condition in which the Russian literary language found itself in the thirties and forties, when Solzhenitsyn began to write as a mature writer, and to imagine the difficulties standing in his creative path.

The Russian literary language of the thirties and forties was a fettered language. Alas, many literary scholars and critics forget this either deliberately or accidentally.

At the same time no one should ignore the interconnections within the language-consciousness-freedom triad. The interdependence of linguistic consciousness and the social life was always particularly and persistently emphasized by Marxism. For example, Marx is the author of this excellent and comprehensive statement about the damage done to literary creativity under conditions of political restraint. It is taken from his "Comments on the Latest Prussian Censorship Instruction" (the italics are his):

"Style is the man." Indeed! The law allows me to write, only I must write not in *my own personal style,* but in some other. I have the right to reveal the face of my mind but I must give it *the prescribed look.* What man of honor would not blush at this demand?...

You are delighted with the amazing variety, the inexhaustible wealth of nature. You do not demand that the rose have the aroma of a violet, why then do you demand that the greatest wealth of all—*the mind*—exist only in one form? I may be a humorist, but the law orders me to write seriously. I may be forward, but the law orders a modest style for me. *Gray on gray*—that is the only permissible color of this *freedom.* Each dewdrop illuminated by the sun pours forth an inexhaustible play of color, but the spiritual sun, no matter in how many individuals and in what objects it may be refracted, must produce only one, only the official color. (6)

Thus the writer becomes victim to *a most terrible terrorism....* The laws which make the main criteria *not actions as such but the sentiments of the person who acts* are nothing but *positive sanctions of lawlessness.* It is better to shave one's beard off as was done by a well-known Russian czar..., rather than to make the criteria for such an action the beliefs by which I wear a beard. (14)

"Rara temporum felicitas, ubi quae velis sentire et quae sentias dicere licet."[1] (26)

The conditions of censorship in Prussia in the middle of the last century, as discussed by Marx, seem to be a kind of web around the wings of the free word, so to speak, compared to the steel trap ensnaring this word under Stalin's regime. It was not only a matter of necessity for accommodation but one of a tremendous indefinable trauma, inflicted on language by police pressure on individual freedom; also, it was a matter of change in the very psychological bases of linguistic consciousness, which had ceased to oppose this pressure. Was it worth it, for example, to restructure word meanings so that the absence of any guarantees of civil freedom is called "the most democratic constitition in the world," so that the impossibility of electing a governing body is "by the freest of elections," so that the poverty of the countryside is named "the abundance of the Kolkhoz," and so forth? All this in an uninterrupted, deafening repetition in spite of what the other founder of Marxism, Engels, wrote in his work *The Origins of the Family, Private Property, and Government:* "Calling a broom a mammal will not make it sprout milk glands."

A fettered language becomes impoverished like a river in a dry spell—in width and in depth. It is quantitatively impoverished—entire word layers drop out as, for example, in the field of religious consciousness, in non-Marxist philosophy and morals, in nonmaterialistic aesthetics, in nonparty sociology, etc. It falls into decay qualitatively as well, because under constant pressure and control its wealth of synonyms becomes depleted; moreover, its very life-giving force dries up and the very soul of the language is distorted and destroyed. In place of living truth and openness comes the lifelessness and wretchedness of the cliché.

I kak pčely v ul'e opustelom,
Durno paxnut mertvye slova.[2]

(And like bees in a deserted hive, dead words smell bad.)

An unprecedented quantity of lexical and phraseological clichés (certainly some examples include the superlatives used in the description of Soviet reality: *selfless,* "the selfless dedication of the Party"; *majestic,* "the majestic construction changing the face of the earth"; *unprecedented,* "the unprecedented sweep of Soviet construction," etc.) fill not only newspaper columns and journals but the pages of stories and novels, and they begin to appear natural and inescapable.[3]

Now, to bring forth out of the bygone "thaw" years a small illustration from the journal *Youth* (no. 7, 1961)—an essay by N. Dolinina called "At Our Grammar School." A student has composed a sketch about a school gathering. He is an aspiring journalist. He writes:

> The participants gathered together long before the start of the party dedicated to the creative work of Russia's leading literary figure, Lev Tolstoy. The colorfully decorated hall was overcrowded. With unabated interest the audience listened to the remarkable lines of the genius of Russian literature, etc.
>
> "Why do you write such an untruth?" the teacher asks Tolik. "Why, there were very few people there at the beginning, and the hall was noisy."
>
> Tolik remained silent.
>
> "And then . . . don't you have any words of your own? What do you mean by 'colorfully decorated hall,' 'with unabated interest'?"
>
> "But what else could I do?" asked Tolik disdainfully. "For my own words I could get a good smack."

To this day the pages of Soviet periodicals are gaudy with traditional superlatives. Here are several headlines at random from two recent issues of the *Literaturnaja Gazeta:* "The Word Ringing Like Steel," "The Heirs of Those Who Conquered the Heavens," "Creation of the Future," "Creators of a New World [Communists]," "The Heart of the Epoch [the Communist Party]."

Lydia Chukovsky writes about this in a letter that appeared in the *Literaturnaja Gazeta* among the articles against Solzhenitsyn. "Not ideas but successions of words," she wrote. "If it is dedication, then it is selfless; if it is loyalty, then it is boundless; if it is a wave of slander, then it is turbid; if it is a rebuff, then it is worthwhile.... Not labor of thought, but a mechanical rearrangement of marks" (6: 122).

Writes Solzhenitsyn, "... let us note that we express ourselves with the least number of repetitious words" (5: 265).

At the basis of linguistic consciousness, which by its own nonfreedom becomes imprisoned by clichés, is, understandably, hypocrisy; and this hypocrisy, or this inevitability, in the words of Vinnichenko, "to lie the truth," snuffs out any talent and illumination in literary creativity.

In contrast to reinterpreting the idea of truth ("Our writer affirms not a faceless, classless truth but our Soviet, communist truth," wrote the newspaper *Pravda* in 1963), Solzhenitsyn presents, as it were, a creatively more organic, a warmer, more personal idea of sincerity—"a merciless sincerity," so named by the Soviet writer N. Asanov.

It is no mere coincidence that in *Cancer Ward* one of the young patients, Dyoma, reads the December 1953 issue of *Novyj Mir,* which contains the article by Pomerantzev, "On Sincerity in Literature":

> "Here is an interesting article," said Dyoma significantly.
> "What about?"
> "About sincerity!" he answered. "About the fact that literature without sincerity...." (2: 55)

Dyoma does not say anything further; an ellipsis follows. But the reader remembers the message of this article, which in its time brought on a wave of official criticism. Pomerantzev observed the absence of sincerity in the works of Soviet writers, clichés and artificiality in many literary works which he called "extracts from newspaper columns." "I am dissatisfied," he wrote, "with the mechanical din in literature, the monotony of it." The history of literature, in his opinion, had demonstrated that writers not only preached but confessed to the reader. Our literature does not need "sermons but confessions," he affirmed. "The degree of sincerity, that is, the spontaneity of things, should be the first measure of value. Sincerity is the basic component among those gifts that total up to what we call talent."

"It is impossible to substitute the truthful expression of reality in its revolutionary course with abstract sincerity," the critic Yermilov answered Pomerantzev in *Pravda*. "The most important element of a work of art is not sincerity but ideology."

This argument is reflected in *Cancer Ward* quite fully. In the chapter entitled "The Shadows Go Their Way" Dyomka asks Rusanov's daughter, Avieta, a poetess and future journalist, who has been brought up according to *Pravda* editorials:

> "Please, tell me what you think about the demand for sincerity in literature?"
> What's that? What did you say?" said Avieta turning quickly toward him. . . . That wretched "sincerity" again! It's wormed its way in here too. They got rid of an entire editorial staff for this sincerity and it's back again.

And she answers like a true follower of Yermilov:

> "The one who wrote the article turned everything inside out and didn't think things through. Sincerity cannot be the chief criterion for judging a book. If an author expresses incorrect ideas or alien attitudes, sincerity only aggravates the harm that work does. Sincerity is harmful. Subjective sincerity can turn out to be against the truthful presentation of life." (2: 321)

And so on.

Sincerity—merciless, courageous, and honest—is the essence of Solzhenitsyn's literary creations, a sincerity in which poetic and ethical elements merge into one definitive feature of his style and craft.

But sincerity demands the categorical rejection of clichés and hypocrisy, which had become rooted in the language of the literature contemporary to Solzhenitsyn. He had to find an equivalent mode of expression for sincerity. The writer who regards his creation as his mission no doubt autobiographically relives the lines from Pushkin's "Prophet" concerning language inspired from above.

I on k ustam moim prinik,
I vyrval grešnyj moj jazyk,
I prazdnoslovnyj, i lukavyj,
I žalo mudryja zmei
V usta zameršie moi
Vložil desniceju krovavoj.

(He bent down to my mouth and tore out my tongue, sinful and deceitful, and given to idle talk; and with his right hand he inserted the sting of a wise serpent into my benumbed mouth.)

There was a need to find if not a "sting" (even though Solzhenitsyn uses satire), then a language which, as Gogol wrote "tore itself from the very heart, . . . seethed and surged," a language with a peculiar inner brilliance, clarity, and warmth—spontaneous and more sincere.

Solzhenitsyn discovered this language by turning to the colloquial conversational language, in an original oral *počvennost'*—just as some time ago Dostoevsky after four years in prison found a redefinition of his views in *počvennost'*.

In 1965 Solzhenitsyn participated in a discussion about stylistics in the modern Russian language. His article "It Is Not Customary to Whiten Cabbage Soup with Tar but with Sour Cream" was published in the *Literaturnaja Gazeta* (no. 31). The vocabulary and character of actual speech do not contain the defects of the modern written language, he declared in this article. "This gives us a not quite impoverished source to suffuse, to freshen, to resurrect our lines. It is not too late to improve the character of our written (authorial!) language, in order to bring back to it a folkish, idiomatic lightness and freedom," he writes.

This emancipation and resurrection of verbal creation is presented in Solzhenitsyn's prose both abundandly and convincingly.

2

In the majority of published analyses of Solzhenitsyn's books consideration of his language is limited to an examination of lexical innovations, insofar as the notions "vocabulary" and "language" are synonymous in the minds of these writers. However, a fascination for unusual, chiefly dialect words and neologisms, has been characteristic of many writers even before Solzhenitsyn, although no one called them innovators for this.

Solzhenitsyn's turning to popular speech is not of course confined to its vocabulary. It includes the entire syntactic-stylistic system, rhythm, sound—the entire structure of oral expression. From popular speech Solzhenitsyn borrows its spontaneity, its emotional overtones, its figurative expression. Pushkin once said that Karamzin restored freedom to the Russian language, "turning it towards the living sources of popular speech."[4] No comparison intended, one can say something close to this about Solzhenitsyn: his verbal innovation makes him the creator of a new style of modern prose.

In his efforts to enliven and enrich the lexicon of the literary language Solzhenitsyn uses the dictionary of Dahl widely. From past and local parlance he recovers lost and forgotten expressions, which, he says, "although not alive in the modern conversational language, are used by the author in such a comprehensible way that they can be suited to the speakers, drawn attention to, and thus be returned to the language."

Apparently, these restorations can be rejected only in the event that, beside their contemporary synonyms, they do not manifest their distinctive semantic-functional content or, even worse, have something in common with some secondary concepts, thereby forcing us to take up the dictionary.

Much more often, however, a restored word contains something difficult to define but distinctly new in its semantic breadth and sound. For example, found in Dahl is the word *vbirčivo,* meaning "very attentively": "slušal vbirčivo," "vbirčivo imi dyšal"—is this word not fresher than the ordinary *vnimatel'no* ("attentively") or *žadno* ("greedily")?

Other sources of innovation in vocabulary are (1) words "overheard" by the author in living conversational surroundings and (2) "his own" word creations. Sometimes it is difficult to distinguish between these two sources, as it used to be in Leskov's work. In his investigation of Leskov's *skaz*[5] academician A. S. Orlov wrote: "It is difficult to say which of the expressions the author actually heard and which were composed by him in a style corresponding to an actual existing model."

This is very true also with respect to Solzhenitsyn. Both the "over-

heard'' and "his own" expressions are engendered in his search for
novelty. The search is often experimental, that is, it is doomed to failure
even if only in certain instances. As with the borrowings from Dahl's
dictionary, there are some not so successful discoveries by Solzhenitsyn.

But at times this word selection is so natural, simply because the
substitutions in the overwhelming majority of cases are valuable finds,
thanks to their own originality, which carries within itself a great expressiveness, in other words, a great spontaneity of communication.
After all, spontaneity and sincerity are kindred spirits.

Some examples: *nedokurok* ("a cigarette butt"), *soldjagi* ("soldiers"), *zlodenjata* ("evil brood"), *skrest' e dorog* ("a road crossing"),
prilepina ("tumor"), *malen'kie kvanty kaši* ("tiny quanta of kasha"),
and many others.

In the aforementioned article on the modern literary language, Solzhenitsyn notes in the language an abundance of verbal nouns ending in
-enie, which indicates bookishness. "When these nouns ending in *-enie*
pile up four or five at a time, your tongue gets twisted and you almost
develop a toothache," he writes. This complaint has been uttered before
him by writers who tried to avoid the stifling Slavonic bookishness in
the living language. "I weaned Pilnyak away from verbs in *-enie,"*
wrote Remizov, for example. "But I can't get away from participles
myself. I called my book *Pljašuščij Demon* but in Russian it should be
Pljašet Demon. I translated it into *Le Démon Dançant.*"[6]

The folkishness of the oral orientation animates an entire group of
prefixed and suffixed word formations, imparting to them, in some
degree or another, the expressiveness of conversational spontaneity.
This natural way of conveying a more intense level of activity is unusual
in the system of "neutral" authorial commentary: *isperepološit' sja* ("to
get extremely panicky"; the prefix *is* conveys the notion of doing something to an extreme), *rasstaryvat' sja* ("to try very hard"; the prefix *ras*
conveys intensity); the endearing forms: *junen'kaja* (from *junyj*—
"youthful"), *xrupen'kaja* (from *xrupkij*—"fragile"), *šelomok* (from
šelom, šlem—"helmet").

Sometimes the new word introduced by Solzhenitsyn contains such a
charge of emotional and authorial suggestiveness that it illuminates the
whole expression, thus determining its stylistic and semantic system.
There is, for example, the word *ljapat',* in the sense of doing something

haphazardly, very carelessly, and then there is the verb pair *lepit'* — *slepit'*, "to build" or "to shape." Solzhenitsyn creates the hybrid *sljapit'*, and his new word becomes so suggestive in context (the example is taken from his "City on the Neva"): "Kakoe sčast'e, čto zdes' ničego nel'zja postroit'!—ni konditerskogo neboskreba vtisnut' v Nevskij, ni pjatietažnuju korobku *sljapit'* u kanala Griboedova" (5: 226) (What luck! It is not permissible to build anything here—you couldn't squeeze a confectioner's skyscraper into Nevsky Prospect, you couldn't slap together a five-story box on the Griboedov Canal).

At other times the conversational word is not itself new but is used in such a surprising metaphorical context that it takes on a whole new charge of expressiveness. For example: "Zotov predstavil sebe Samokurova—i v nem *zabul'kalo*" (Zotov imagined Samokurov—and he began to choke) (from "Incident at Krechetovka Station"); or "I Pavla Nikolaeviča *zaščipalo*, i ponjal on, čto sovsem otmaxnut'sja ot smerti ne vyxodit" (Something tweaked inside Pavel Nikolaevich, and he realized that he would not be able to dismiss death entirely) (from *Cancer Ward*); or in the description of a character's happy mood: "A v grudi tak perepolaskivalo!" (Something in his chest seemed to rinse over) (from *Cancer Ward*).

Conversational spontaneity is the source of the following epithets, which have different expressive possibilities—*peredyxannyj vozdux* ("stale, used-up air"), *stomivšij s nog poceluj* ("a kiss that knocks one off one's feet"), *zaezžennyj očkami nos* ("a nose worn out by glasses"—from *zaezžennaja lošad'*, "a worn-out horse"), *perešiblennaja sud'ba* ("a crushed fate"), *dolgozvannoe sčast'e* ("a long called for happiness"), *čutkonosyj stukač* ("stool pigeon with a sensitive nose"), and others.

The forms of popular phraseology were richly represented even in Solzhenitsyn's first novel (its language will be discussed in the following chapter); in the same work his partiality for proverbial expressions, including original ones, was evident. It is interesting that at a conference of the Secretariat of the Soviet Writers' Union Solzhenitsyn answered his critics in proverbs. "Do not love the opportunist, love the debator." "He who has honeyed words on his lips does not always wish you well," he said.

The tendency to rely on proverbs as on folk wisdom, the native ore of the popular language, is felt especially in the last novel, *August 1914*. There Solzhenitsyn sometimes uses proverbs as types of "reverse epigraphs." They close the chapter, as if to summarize the author's evaluation of what has been narrated. For example, the sixty-third chapter of the novel concerns the czar's reply to the grand duke's report on the destruction of Samsonov's army—the czar has ordered a miraculous icon to be brought to headquarters. The chapter ends with the proverb: "Praying kneads no dough."

3

Now, the other structural features of Solzhenitsyn's language.

"The most captious selection of Russian words is still far from the Russian idiom. Much more important is the Russian *sklad*—the Russian construction of phrases," writes Solzhenitsyn in his article (5: 265) as he brings out Dahl's warning. "In the non-Russian turn of phrase not only the arms and legs of our words are amputated, but also the tongue—it stiffens and grows dumb."

Sklad, according to Dahl, "is the capability of a language to combine words." "The beauty, or rather the goodness, of a language," said Lev Tolstoy, "can be examined in two ways—with respect to the words used, and with respect to their combinations."

Solzhenitsyn understands *sklad* as a "way of governing words through words, their connections, their positions in a phrase, the intonational transitions between them" (5: 264). In other words, they are a structural-stylistic form of communication. This form should reflect the spirit of an oral *počvennost'*.

In Solzhenitsyn's first work, *One Day in the Life of Ivan Denisovich,* the slang-conversational features of the work are explained by the image of the narrator.[7] But in the novel *Cancer Ward* we find, for example, these sentences as authorial commentary on the autobiographical hero, Kostoglotov: "on tak uxo priklonjal, čtoby gordosti ne uščerbnut'— slušal vbirčivo, a vrode ne očen' eto emu i nužno" (2: 136) (he lent an ear, no loss to his pride. He soaked up everything he could, pretending all the time that there was no real reason for doing so). Here not only the expressions *priklonjal* ("to lend an ear"), *vbirčivo* ("attentively"), *gordosti ne uščerbnut'* ("no loss to his pride") but the composition and intonation of the sentence belong entirely to the *sklad* of popular speech.

To name or to enumerate all the separate elements of this *sklad* or phraseology would probably be impossible—rather, what is needed here is the reader's sensitivity and his direct contact with the word. In any case several types of sentence construction, intonation, and rhythm peculiar to the lightness and freedom of oral speech can be noted:

(*a*) A liberal, "ungrammatical" word order in a phrase, a conversational shortening of different word groups where grammar would demand a more diffuse style: "A vygljadel Zotov sebe rabotu ešče takuju" (1: 149–150) (But Zotov found himself some other such work).

(*b*) A binary phrase construction, as often it occurs in a proverb—a caesura in the middle, and the intonation often rises and then falls. But always a contrast. "If one is forever cautious, can one remain a human being?" (3: 8).

"Any fool can bomb a train, but just try sorting out the mess" (1: 148).

(*c*) The formation and coupling of clauses with internally unproductive repetitions, rhythmic irregularities, and sometimes internal rhyme, which almost transmits the very "movement" of oral communication. The examples are two of many. "I šli goda, kak plyla voda. . . . V sorok pervom ne vzjali na vojnu Faddeja iz-za slepoty . . . (1: 216) (And the years passed as the water flowed. . . . In forty-one Faddei was not called to war because of bad eyesight . . .). "Ljutyj knjaz', zlodej kosoglazyj, zaxvatil ozero: von dača ego kupal'nja ego. Zlodenjata lovjat rybu, b'jut utok s lodki. Sperva sinij dymok nad ozerom, a pogodja—vystrel" (5: 222) (A fierce prince, a cross-eyed villain, has captured the lake; there is his summer cottage, there is his bathhouse. His evil brood goes fishing there, shoots duck from his boat. First a wisp of blue smoke over the lake, then in a moment—the shot).

Speaking not of *sklad* but of the new style—the innovation in Solzhenitsyn's stylistic manner as a whole—one unusually important literary device must be mentioned. This very device significantly creates that spontaneous, sincere, and intelligible tonality of oral communication that is perceived as the chief distinction of Solzhenitsyn's prose.

When introducing a character's speech, Solzhenitsyn almost plunges his story into the speech pattern of that character. This device slightly resembles the form of "indirect speech," but in Solzhenitsyn's case the device is structurally quite different. It is not simply two or three of the character's words or expressions that sprinkle the author's words, but a kind of organic fusion between the language of the author and that of the dialogue. This is based on the fact that both of these languages (the author's and the character's) are inspired by the folk elements of speech. From the standpoint of figurative expressiveness this can be regarded as a device of oral *ostranenie*.[8]

In Solzhenitsyn's books there are quite a few characters who from time to time become the author's focal point. Thus a very interesting and original polyphony of narrative speech emerges.

Here, for example, is a description of Matryona in the story "Matryona's Home"; the author almost imitates his heroine in the choice of words, phrase composition, and intonation:

A delo vsjakoe načinala "s Bogom!" i mne vsjakij raz "s Bogom" norovila skazat', kogda ja šel v školu.... Viseli v izbe ikony. Zabudni stojali oni temnye, a vo vremja vsenoščnoj i s utra po prazdnikam zažigala Matrena lampadku. (1: 210)

(And whatever she did began with "God bless!" and to me she tried to say "God bless you!" every time I set out for school.... There were icons in the cottage. On ordinary days they were dark, but during vespers and on feastdays Matryona would light the icon lamp.)

Or—in *The First Circle*—the yardkeeper Spiridon: "Doma u sebja mužik nezaležlivyj, v tjur'me Spiridon ne ljubil podxvatyvat'sja v temned'. Iz-pod palki do sveta vstavat'—samoe zloe delo dlja arestanta" (4: 596–597) (At home he was not a lazy peasant; in prison Spiridon did not like getting up in the darkness. To get up before dawn under the lash was the worst thing for a prisoner.)

A rhythmical smoothness analogous to *skaz* quite often accompanies this literary device. The story of the patient Yefrem Podduyev, suffering from cancer of the tongue:

Perebyval on vo mnogix krajax, peredelal propast' raznoj raboty, tam lomal, tam kopal, tam snabžal, a zdes' stroil, ne unižalsja sčitat' niže červonca, ot polulitra ne šatalsja, za vtorym litrom ne tjanulsja—i tak on čuvstvoval sebja i vokrug sebja, čto ni predela, ni rubeža ne postavleno Efremu Podduevu, a vsegda on budet takoj. (2: 111)

(He had been everywhere, done a lot of different jobs, quarried here, dug there, delivered here, built there, didn't stoop to count change under ten rubles, didn't stagger from a fifth and didn't reach out for a second—and so he felt that around him there were no limits, no boundary lines were placed around Efrem Podduyev, and he would always be like that.)

In *August 1914* this stylized polyphonic narration subordinated to the theme being discussed is very distinct. The following deals with the soldier Arsenij (Senka) who accompanies Colonel Vorotyntzev: "Po vsemu okruž'ju toptalas', krylas' i elozila naša soldatnja, i každyj kuju-nebud' Kat'ku brosil, da ne rot razevat', o nej vspominat' Ešče do konca etogo dnja sam li Senka budet živ?'' (239)[9] (Our army trampled, hid and crawled over the whole region, and each one left some sort of Katja behind, and don't stand with your mouth wide open thinking about her. At the end of this day would Senka himself still be alive?).

Then General Samsonov, the central character of the novel—a special kind of magic stands behind the choice of words, the rhythmic phraseology, and the sound pattern of the narrative, and it transmits a monumental image of the commander in the depth of his experience. Samsonov's prayer:

On stojal kolenno, vsej tjažest'ju vdavlivajas' v pol, smotrel na skla-den' vroven' glaz svoix, šeptal, molčal, krestilsja—i menee, i telo ne tak gruzno, i duša ne tak temna: vse tjažkoe i temnoe bezzvučno i nevidimo otpadalo ot nego, otdeljalos', vozgonjalos'—eto Bog na sebja prinimal ot nego tjagoty.... (292)

(He was on his knees, all his weight pressing on the floor, he stared at the icon, level with his eyes. He whispered, hushed, and crossed himself—and the weight of his right arm seemed less with every cross-ing, and his body was not so bulky, and his soul not so dark. All the heaviness and darkness noiselessly, invisibly dropped from him, de-tached itself and sublimated—God had taken his burden upon Himself.)

Sometimes the originality of the style is accompanied by features of onomatopoeia. It is true that their functional ''purpose'' is sometimes difficult to determine even by the author himself, and many researchers tend to stretch their interpretation in these cases. Nevertheless, here is an example. It is perhaps precisely the ''down-to-earth'' quality of the spiritual side of Ensign Lenartovich (*August 1914*), the deserter from the front, that comes across in the alliteration of "z" in such lines:

Sejčas, rtom iz' ev krupitčatuju zemlju u kartofel'nyx klubnej, osypannyx bryzgamizemli ot blizkix pul', uže prostjas' so vsej svoej žizn'ju—neispolnennoj, počti ne načatoj, takojljubimoj žizn'ju! popjatnym červjačnym dviženiem vyelœziv iz beskonečnoj borœdy, ni razu golovu ne otnjav ot zemli, on bespamjatno pobrodil po lesu. . . . (420)

(Now having eaten a mouthful of grainy soil along with the potato tubers which were sprinkled with soil from nearby bullets, he was already saying good-bye to his short life, almost not yet begun, such a beloved life! With a worm-like movement he backed out and, having slipped out of the endless furrow, not once raising his head from the ground, he wandered senselessly through the forest. . . .)

Such are the general observations concerning the structural and stylistic peculiarities of this "new style" of Russian narrative prose that is presented in Solzhenitsyn's works.

Some additional remarks about the poetics of his prose are included in the following chapters.

3

Ivan
Denisovich—
Zotov—Matryona

There will not be, there never was a glittering world!
A foot cloth in the hoar frost, a bandage around your face.
An argument over porridge, the shout of a brigade leader,
Day after day, there's never an end to it.

—A. Solzhenitsyn (6: 307)

1

"It is hard to imagine that only one year ago we did not know the name Solzhenitsyn. It seems that he has been alive in our literature for a long time, and without him it would decidedly be incomplete."

The quotation is taken from V. Lakshin's article "Ivan Denisovich—His Friends and Enemies," the best among the numerous critical responses to this work, at least in the Russian language.[1]

In his analysis Lakshin managed to find and to name the crux of the author's art, that which helped Solzhenitsyn's narrative become a literary event. "Solzhenitsyn," said Lakshin, "writes so that we see and learn about the life of a convict not from the sidelines but from within, 'from him.'"

This "from within" is splendid! It is a pity that polemical themes diverted the author of the article from an investigation of this "from within." It must be pursued.

The contrast between "from the sidelines" and "from within" is seen clearly if we compare *One Day in the Life of Ivan Denisovich* with Solzhenitsyn's play *The Deer and Shalashovka*. Both concern life behind barbed wire. But what a disparity in aspects of artistry!

The four acts (eleven scenes) of the play are full of the speeches and actions of fifty-seven characters. Besides these the following walk-on characters are listed in the author's stage directions: "Workers, Brigade Leaders, Goofoffs, Overseers, Miners, Escort Guards, Tower Guards." Of the fifty-seven speaking parts, twelve belong to guards and free laborers; forty-five are "zeks" (prisoners). The first group is mostly "furniture," the second forty-five are human destinies.

These destinies, however, are not revealed in depth. They flow past the reader-spectator like the sequences of a film. Even the two title destinies—Rodion Nemov, recently from the front, and Lyuba Negnevitzkaya—are drawn with very scanty strokes.

This is the climax: Nemov does not want to share his love with any of the extortionists. This unwillingness signifies the loss of a loved one, signifies a halting place.

> *Lyuba:* . . . We can survive! We can love each other very very secretly. Only promise . . . only agree . . . to share me. With Timofey. I will bring you food to eat!
> *Nemov:* And you could do this? . . .
> *Lyuba:* I could! My brother—can you? Well, reconcile yourself. Why do you have to leave? At least I will see you from a distance.
> *Nemov* (hugs her): Not a bit of you will I share with anybody, my darling Lyuba. (5: 112)

The subtext makes up for the conciseness of the dialogue by completing the unsaid. Here is a reference to the same extortion of love.

> *Third Woman:* The supervisor took Lyuba away to the office.
> *Granya:* What can she do?
> *Second Woman:* Don't you understand? . . . (5: 38)

The old overseer Kolodey shakes out the books from the old Belgian, Gontuar's suitcase.

> *Gontuar:* Who do my books bother? Books are not forbidden.
> *Kolodey:* Wha-at, this is not forbidden? Who told you that books are not forbidden!

This entire eerie mosaic of prison life and wickedness is viewed as if through binoculars. The author's presence is not felt according to the nature of the genre. But we sense his gaze—also from the sidelines—in the choice and distribution of characters, colors, and in the arrangement of accents. For example, in this telling contrast in the author's stage directions that open the final scene of the play: "Twilight. The prisoners crowd around the workers' area behind the barbed wire. Motionless, they look this way into the living area. About thirty persons already questioned sit on the ground in the middle of the yard in a group with their things. A stream of light from a projector shines on a newly hung poster: "People are the most valuable capital. J. Stalin' " (5: 119).

Now, *One Day in the Life of Ivan Denisovich:* here there is no distance between the eye and the stage; there is no angle of vision, no author-director somewhere on the sidelines.

Suddenly someone takes the reader firmly by the hand, leads him behind the barbed wire and into a day of prison life. And, without releasing the reader's hand, he comments upon this day in a confidential manner that charms the reader. For in this manner there is neither fear, nor insecurity, nor twaddle.

This is exposing "from within."

To understand the nature of this means to clarify the image of this "someone"—the narrator, with whose eyes the reader watches the events of the day—the zeks, the friskings, the conflicts, the squads. This image is revealed first of all in the language of the work.

The presence of the narrator and the spoken quality of the narrative constitute the features of *skaz*. In Solzhenitsyn's narrative the spoken style is interspersed with information in a formal literary style. It is of course the author himself who sits at a desk and describes, for example, the naval captain Buinovsky. "A guilty smile parted the chapped lips of the captain who had sailed around Europe and the Great Northern Route. And he bent down, happy over the half scoop of thin oatmeal— no grease, just oats and water" (1: 62).

Also, many of the novel's dialogues are given not in the spoken style common for *skaz,* but with precise verbal characteristics peculiar to the speaker. For example, Tzesar and Buinovsky argue about the film *The Battleship Potemkin.*

"Yes. . . . But navy life is a little bit doll-like there."
"You see, we have been spoiled by modern screen techniques. . . ."

However, the principal element that prevails in the narrative is oral speech—the language of *skaz,* the roots of which are found in an oral *počvennost'* in daily, historical, and dialect layers of folk speech— primarily in ordinary conversation.

The words are from common speech. Here the common speech belongs to a particular locale; it includes prison camp jargon: *oper* ("operations worker"), *popki* ("guards in the watchtowers"), *polkany* ("workers in the messhall"), *pridurki* ("those who manage to get themselves easy assignments"), *šmon* ("search or frisk").

Here is some more generally used slang: *zagnut'* ("to say the improbable"), *vkalyvat'* ("to work zealously"), *maternut'* ("to curse"), *gvozdanut'* ("to nail", in the sense of hit), *nedotyka* ("a dope"), *žituxa* (from *žizn'*—"life"), etc. Here are Solzhenitsyn's "restorations" for the literary language from Dahl's dictionary: *eženen* ("everyday"), *zakalelyj* ("frozen"), *ljut'* ("fierceness"), etc. Finally, the language overheard or created by the author himself in the spirit of common usage, such as: *prigrebat'sja* ("to find fault with"), *podsosat'sja* ("to get a place")—"Tut že i Fetjukov, šakal, podsosalsja" (Immediately then Fetiukov, the jackal, found a place); *razmorčivyj* ("relaxed"), etc.

Colloquial prison camp speech is plentiful: *kačat' prava* ("to demand what is laid down by the law"), *xodit' stučat' k kumu* ("to denounce"). There are many proverbial expressions, composing three different groups: (*a*) borrowings from Dahl, (*b*) parallels to those already existing, (*c*) the original ones, such as: "Two hundred grams [of bread] governs life"and "We'll manage to drag ourselves through the day, but the night is ours."[2]

Various conversational colloquialisms deviate from the usual phrase constructions—"Kotoryj brigadir umnyj—tot na procentovku nalegaet. S ej kormimsja" (That brigade leader is smart who presses upon the percentage norm. With it we feed ourselves). The features of the folklore style are present in descriptions—"Dolgo li, korotko li—vot vse tri okna tolem zašili" (Whether for long or for only a while, we mend all three windows with roofing felt). "Solnce vzošlo krasnoe, mglistoe nad pustoj zonoj: gde ščity sbornyx domov snegom zaneseny, gde kladka kamennaja načataja! . . ." (The sun rose red, hazy above the empty zone: where the snow-screens of prefabricated homes were covered with snow, where the beginnings of a stone wall . . .). A folkish type of comparison—"They surrounded the stove, as if it were a woman; they all crept up to hug it."

Intonations, rhythms, and interruptions typical of *skaz* spring up as if to reflect the very breathing of the narrator:

> Tak on i ždal, i vse ždali tak: esli pjat' voskresenij v mesjace, to tri dajut, a dva na rabotu gonjat. Tak on i ždal, a uslyšal—povelo vsju dušu, perekrivilo: voskresen'ice-to krovnoe komu ne žalko? (1: 102)

> (It was just as he expected, and everyone else expected it too. If there were five Sundays in the month, they gave you three and sent you to work on the other two. It was just as he expected, but when he heard it his soul became cramped and distorted. Who is not sorry about the loss of a sweet Sunday?)

In summary, the vocal image of a storyteller is merged with the traits of a simple worker with a hard life. The reader readily identifies this storyteller with Ivan Denisovich himself.

This dual image of the narrator is nowhere split by the grammatical "I." On the contrary, in certain places the concept of "we" (understood in Russian) is emphasized.

> ... The number spells nothing but trouble for *us*.[3]
> The thirty-eighth, of course, wouldn't let any stranger near their stove. ... Never mind, *we'll* sit here in the corner. It's not so bad. (1: 37)

> "Mo-ortar," echoes Shukov. ... *We* have to pull the string to a higher row. Forget it, *we'll* lay one row without a string. (1: 79)

Who is included in this "we" along with Ivan Denisovich? Of course, the author himself is reincarnated in the hard-working narrator. The last quote, which deals with stone masonry is, moreover, an autobiographical confirmation of this—Solzhenitsyn worked as a stone mason in the prison camp at Karanda.

This reincarnation creates a mode of exceptional vocal richness. Who indeed would attribute this knowledge of Dahl's dictionary, this aphoristic judgment, this generous speech imagery, to a kolkhoz storyteller? In this mode two "carriers of the author's appraisal"[4] seem to merge, and the language of both is based on the folk idiom.

The process of reincarnation—the transition from a literary or written style to a spoken, colloquial one—is easy to trace. Here is a segment; the *skaz* style is set off from the "written" by italics.

Brigady sideli za stolami ili tolkalis' v proxodax, ždali, kogda mesta osvobodjatsja. Prolikajas' čerez tesnotu, ot každoj brigady rabotjagi po dva, po tri nosili na derevjannyx podnosax miski s balandoj i kašej i iskali dlja nix mesta na stolax. *I vse ravno, ne slyšit, obalduj, spina elovaja, na tebe, tolknul podnos. Ples' ples'! Rukoj ego svobodnoj—po šee, po šee! Pravil'no! Ne stoj na dorogo, ne vysmatrivaj, gde podlizat'.* (1: 13)

(The squads sat at the table or pressed closely together in the aisles, they were waiting for seats to become available. Shouting above the crush, two or three men from each squad were carrying bowls of stew and oatmeal on wooden trays and trying to find room for them on the tables. *And anyway, he doesn't hear, this stiff necked idiot! There, he bumped the tray! Splash, splash! You have a hand free—hit him on the neck, on the neck! That's it! Don't stand there blocking the way, looking for something to swipe.*)

The author's immersion in the spoken manner of a prison camp worker is the very basis for the illustration of Ivan Denisovich's "one day" *from within,* about which Lakshin wrote. It is the nature of the emotion and expressiveness contained in the illustration.

Turning to an oral *počvennost'* style establishes the story's tonal directness and sincerity, which charms the reader. This tonality proves to be, at the same time, both an aesthetic element because it precludes verbosity, and with the absolute compactness of its literary expression it imparts to a cursory observation or to the minutest details an almost symbolic depth and significance.

The simplicity and confidentiality of the story give a visual quality, a luminescence, to the scenes—in the barracks, the mess hall, the search areas, in the construction of TEC (Technical Electric Stations),[5] in the plasticity and colorings of Buinovsky, Tzesar, Fetiukov, and others from Shukov's environment.

And most of all, the character of Ivan Denisovich himself. Perhaps only a line—"Then Shukhov took his hat from his shaved head, no matter how cold it was he could not allow himself to eat with his hat on . . ."—conveys to the reader Ivan Denisovich's inner comeliness, which has inspired critics to associate him with Tolstoy's Platon Karataev.

The simplicity and sincerity of the narrative style, found in the folk quality of language, is extended by Solzhenitsyn to other of his structurally more complicated works.

2

Well, there's vigilance now. What can you do?...
                              —"An Incident at Krechetovka Station"

It is pouring rain.

"... since yesterday the cold rain has been pouring down without stopping, so that one wonders where so much water comes from in the sky."

Flooded with streams of water, which make the rails glisten even at dusk, the Krechetovka station was an almost allegorical picture of the nervousness at the rear guard with all its bustle and disturbances.

And no less suggestive are the figures attending to its feverish life: The record keeper of Aunt Frosya's train car—she has the firm belief that one should exchange potato cakes for soap and silk stockings with those "snouty" evacuees passing through the station ("The DP's are just the ones you should take things from. They've got material. They've got suits"). Then there is the very picturesque old man Kordubailo, a line foreman, about whom critics could write pages. The *počvennost'* of his personality and of the sly wisdom in his lines is presented so strongly. The "komsomolka" on military duty, Valya, with her fresh, pale pink lips is a little in love with Zotov, an assistant to the military commander at the station. And there is Vasya Zotov himself, the main character of the story.

Zotov's character is sketched in very telling details: He "straightened his glasses, giving a stern expression to his not so stern face." "Taking off his glasses, his head became somewhat childish...." And in another place Valya looks at his "comically set-off ears, his snub nose, and his pale blue eyes, flecked with gray." He has, we discover, a chubby palm with short fat fingers, which he often rubs.

Zotov is pedantic, almost childishly so. And as he himself observes, his is "a character with inclinations to systematize." His wife has remained in the area occupied by the Germans, but his notion of morality is high—he is even slightly afraid of women, even of his young dispatcher.

Still greater is Zotov's feeling of duty. To the party: his only reading in the evening now is a volume of Marx's *Das Kapital,* which according to his calculations should make him "invincible, invulnerable, and irrefutable in any battle of ideas." Civic duty: he finds it troublesome that instead of being needed at the front, he is needed at home; he worries about the unlucky course of the war. However, he regards even the incipience of critical thoughts as criminal ("It would be an insult to the almighty, all-knowing Father and Teacher, who is always in his place and foresees all," etc.).

Gradually the reader is filled with a speechless sympathy for Zotov and agrees with Valya, who thought that "at work he was caustic, this Vasil Vasilich, but not mean. And what especially pleased her—he was a man who was not unduly familiar, but polite."

And now, when we have gone through half of the story, the incident itself occurs. Tveritinov, who has been separated from his unit, appears at the commandant's office.

Well, this old, poorly dressed, unshaven actor, with a greasy old Red Army sack in hand, also instantly wins over the reader. Above all, this occurs through Zotov's perception of him. Zotov likes his voice— "rich, low, aristocratically restrained, so as not to boast." His manner of speaking is pleasant, and his smile—"This eccentric man had a very likeable, open-hearted smile," he thinks.

Both, sympathetic toward each other, sit facing each other; one with the firm desire to help a man who is in trouble, the other worn out by the warmth of the room and by inhaling the cigarettes he has borrowed from Zotov.

The reader is so anxiously awaiting a satisfactory conclusion to the story that he perhaps does not notice the dissonance, delicately woven into the placidity of the scene by the author. The conversation turns to the year 1937—how contrasting are the attitudes of each of them! For one this is the year of the madness of Stalin's terror; for the other it is the year of civil war in Spain and the Soviets' secret intervention in it.

"... Yes, in general it is dangerous for us to raise questions," said Tveritinov.

"During wartime, of course."

"But it was true even before the war."

"Is that so? I didn't notice it."

"It was," Tveritinov squinted a little. "After '37."

"And what about '37?" Zotov was surprised. "What happened in '37? The war in Spain?"

"Oh no...." Tveritinov said, again with the same guilty smile and downcast eyes. "No...." (1: 174)

So far both of them do not notice the dissonance, and almost lyrical pauses spring up in their conversation. Tveritinov shows Zotov a photograph of his daughter ("Zotov liked the girl very much, his expression relaxed"). Something in the nature of an interior monologue accompanies Zotov's examination of the photograph; even the style of the monologue betrays how touched he is (1: 179)—"at this point he did not hold back his sympathy for this even-tempered fellow. He had been right in taking an instant liking to him."

And suddenly.... Suddenly Tveritinov cannot remember what Stalingrad had been called before its renaming. And we read: "everything burst and suddenly froze in Zotov. Is it possible? A Soviet man— and he doesn't know Stalingrad? That means he is not ours. He is a plant! An agent!... This is vigilance. What should I do now? What now?" (1: 186).

And Zotov turns in this fellow, to whom he had taken a liking, to the local unit of the NKVD.

"What are you doing? What are you doing?" screamed Tveritinov in a voice as resonant as a bell. "Why, *this cannot be corrected!*"

"Don't worry, don't worry," Zotov tried to soothe him, as he groped for the threshold of the passageway with his foot. "You will only have to *explain one minor question....*"

And he went out. (1: 192)

The creative-experiential weight of Solzhenitsyn's works lies not only in the fact that he chooses such tragic events from the recent past as subject matter but that he extends these events into our times as if testing their life stability, their contemporary vitality.

Vigilance! How did this fetish of vigilance—the springboard for denunciation and treachery—take shape in the consciousness of a people?

In a dictionary published in the thirties by the USSR Academy of Sciences under the editorship of Ushakov, the word *nedonositel'stvo* ("noninformation") is included with the definition "A misdemeanor, a crime, involving the non-informing of something; nedonositel' (noninformer)—an individual guilty of noninforming."

The poem "Pavlik Morozov" by Stepan Shchipachev, published in the journal *Znamya* (no. 6, 1950), must be considered the apotheosis of the vigilance theme in postrevolutionary literature. It is a poem which, as the saying goes, "you cannot toss one word out of" no matter how vile it sounds; otherwise we cannot judge the whole.

Pavlik, a village teenager, is depressed by the fact that his father, Trifon, shields village kulaks, who do not want to give their grain to the government, and he refuses to inform the authorities about them:

> Pavlik i slyšlat' ne možet
> Teper' o svoem otce,
> Brovej ne sdvinuv strože,
> Ne izmenivšis' v lice.

(Pavlik cannot hear of his father now without knitting his brows and changing the look on his face.)

So Pavlik informs on his father. As an example of high consciousness, the voice of filial love is drowned out by the greatness of another, much more significant fatherhood:

> Otec—dorogoe slovo!
> V nem nežnost', v nem i surovost'.
> Stalinu, soveršaja
> Vsej žizni svoej povorot,
> Ljubov' svoju vyražaet
> Etim slovom narod. . . .

(Father is a dear word! In it is tenderness, in it sternness. To Stalin, who achieved the transformation of his entire life, the people express their love with this word. . . .)

How firm is this reflex of absolute distrust and voluntary watchfulness in people?

Solzhenitsyn believes in man. His Zotov, having informed the authorities "I am herewith sending you the prisoner Tveritinov, Igor De-mentyevich, who alleges..." etc., can no longer find complete spiritual peace,

> Several days passed. The holiday came and went.
> But Zotov could not erase the memory of the man with such a remark-
> able smile and the snapshot of his daughter in a little striped dress.
> Surely he had done everything as he should have.
> Yes, but.... (1: 193)

This "Yes, but..." is remarkable. This is the substance of the past that Solzhenitsyn brings into the actual conditions of our modern life. This "criterion," the application of which is much broader than the basic conflict in the plot of the story, constitutes its inner, so significantly human theme.

3

The people who are at peace with their consciences always have good faces.

—"Matryona's Home"

The image of Matryona is so much in the center of Solzhenitsyn's story that our analysis should begin directly with it.

An émigré observer of Russian literature once said in a private conversation: "For me Matryona is the most brilliant image of the peasant woman in all of the Russian literature I have read."

Instead of objecting to this, I would like to consider the matter more carefully. Wherein lies the impressive power of this character? Of the story itself?

After several sentences designed to alert the reader (a railroad accident is hinted at—it is the one in which Matryona dies) the narrator describes his return from a great distance away, where he "delayed his return for ten years or so," and his search for asylum—"I just wanted to crawl away and lose myself in the very heartland of Russia—if there were such a place."

First-person narrative is a usual thing, but there is something special in the "I" of this story that wins the reader over. Perhaps it is the easily discernible autobiographical quality of this "I" that summons our sympathy. Perhaps it is the narrative manner itself, very plain and sincere, in which everything is told.

Perhaps, finally, it is the warmth with which the narrator looks upon the destitute village of Talnovo, Matryona's poor utensils, Matryona herself, sick and ordered around by everyone; the warmth with which, after having settled down in her house, he describes her unchanging good-will, openheartedness, and the radiant smile on her kind face. The reader feels that this is no hunter with a gun, no essayist with a notebook in his pocket—observers of the lives of others "along one's path" or "on the run." No, the narrator has familiarized himself with this life; he is at home in this half-lit room with fig plants on the benches and mice behind the walls. "At night when Matryona was already asleep and I was working at my table, the quick rustle of mice behind the wallpaper was muffled by the uniform, monotonous, ceaseless rustle of cockroaches behind the partition, like the distant roar of the ocean. But I grew accustomed to it, for there was nothing false or deceptive about it. Their rustling was their life" (1: 201).

The narrator sometimes speaks with the vocabulary and intonations characteristic of Matryona's speech:

> Tak, odnoj utel'noj koze sobrat' bylo sena dlja Matreny—trud velikij. Brala ona s utra mešok i serp i uxodila v mesta, kotorye pomnila, gde trava rosla po obmežkam, po zadoroge, po ostrovkam sredi bolota.... S meška travy polučalos' podsoxšego sena—navil'nik. (1: 206)

> (So collecting hay for one skinny little goat was a lot of work for Matryona. She took her sickle and a sack and early in the morning would set off for the places where she remembered grass was growing—along the edges of the fields on the roadside, on the hummocks in the bog.... From a sackload of grass she got one forkload of dry hay.)

Unhappy in her family life and constantly in need ("at the kolkhoz she worked not for money, but for credit"), Matryona delights the narrator with her limitless unselfishness, her sacrificial readiness to labor not for herself but for others.

Her good qualities especially stand out when contrasted with her kolkhoz surroundings—the pitiless, embittered, even predatory battle with poverty.

There is something fatal in the character of the predatory Faddei,

Matryona's brother-in-law (in the way that character is inserted into the structure of the story). At one time Faddei had been Matryona's fiance; he had been taken prisoner and upon his return found her married to his brother—"he stood on the doorstep," Matryona tells her boarder. "I cried out!. . . . 'If he weren't my own brother,' he said, 'I'd chop up the pair of you.' "

Now Faddei insists that Matryona give up a part of her cottage—the top room—to his daughter. The top room is dismantled, and while transporting the sledge with logs, in her constant readiness to help, Matryona perishes in the catastrophe at the railroad crossing.

The scene of the burial follows: the amazing "laments" for the deceased, and a bit earlier the no less amazing description of the narrator's first night in an empty cottage.

> I lay down leaving the light on. The mice squeaked, almost groaned, all the time racing up and down. My tired mind could not rid itself of an involuntary sense of horror. I had the feeling that Matryona herself was invisibly moving about and bidding farewell to her cottage.
>
> Suddenly in the hallway by the front door I imagined the young black-bearded Faddei with his raised axe.
>
> "If he weren't my own brother, I would chop up the pair of you."
>
> His threat had lain for forty years like a broad-sword in a corner—and it finally struck. . . . (1: 224)

Finally the conclusion, where the sincere tone of the story reaches the lyrical heights of generalization:

> We had all lived alongside her but we hadn't understood that she was the one righteous person without whom, as the saying goes, no village can stand.
>
> Nor any city.
>
> Nor our whole land.

The eerie *počvennost'* of the narrator's "I" is condensed into this conclusion. His painting of good and evil, his sense of discovery, are embodied for him in the character of the story's heroine.

In Dostoevsky's "Diary": "if a person's heart has throbbed even once for the suffering of the people, he will understand and pardon all the impenetrable, alluvial soil, in which our people are buried, and he will be able to discover diamonds in this soil.''

But we can find Matryona's forerunner even closer to our times in Leskov—starting with *Cathedral Folk,* the theme of the righteous man became his main theme. ''I gave the reader positive types of Russian people,'' he said. ''My entire second volume under the title 'Righteous Individuals' portrays the gratifying circumstance of Russian life.''

In his memoirs Leskov gives an account of his dispute with Pisemsky, the author of the novel *A Thousand Souls* and the play *A Bitter Fate.*

''According to you,'' Pisemsky said, ''it is as if one should always write about the good, but brother, I write about what I see, and I see only muck.''

''That is because you have a diseased vision.''

''Maybe . . . but what should I do if I see nothing but abominations in my own and in your soul?''

''From his words,'' notes Leskov, ''I was seized by a fierce uneasiness. I thought 'Can it be that neither in mine, nor in his, nor in any Russian soul there is nothing but rot to be seen?' . . . If without three righteous men, as an old saying goes, a city cannot stand, then how can the entire earth maintain its balance on only the rot that lives in your soul and mine, reader?''

In a sense there is a shade of Leskov in the very spoken structure of the story (''in a sense'' because Solzhenitsyn's artistic use of popular linguistic elements is entirely his own, and one can note only several features of his muse that provide a continuity in this modality of his art) as with Leskov certain local or dialect words are italicized: *kartov'* (''potato''), *sup kartonnyj* (''potato soup''), *nemogluxoj* (''dumb and deaf''), and others; also, the so-called words of folk etymology in Matryona's own language—*razvedka* for *rozetka* (''rosette''), *porcija* for *porca* (''spoilage''), *duel'* (''draft''), etc.; finally, the rhythm and melodiousness of oral narration, which are the ordinary elements of Leskov's *skaz.* For example: ''I poprosila ona [Matrena] u toj vtoroj, zabitoj Matreny—čreva ee uryvoček (ili krovinočku Faddeja?)— mladšuju ix devočku Kiru'' (1: 216) (And she [Matryona] begged the other Matryona for a child of her womb (perhaps because it was Faddei's flesh and blood?)—their youngest daughter, Kira).

It is difficult to agree with Lukacs' conviction in his book on Solzhenitsyn that the depiction of village life in "Matryona's Home" is "very little influenced by Stalinism" and that "An Incident at Krechetovka Station" is more closely tied to this epoch.[6] True, Solzhenitsyn's direct condemnation of the burdens and vulgarities of kolkhoz life is no greater than that of certain contemporaries (Abramov, Mozhaev, Tendryakov, and others). But the reflection of the epoch is profoundly revealed in the story by a significant polarization: the spiritual impoverishment of the enslaved village on the one hand, and on the other—that sought-for, lofty *righteousness,* which the rulers of that epoch could neither approve nor allow. It is this inner theme of the story which was given such a hostile reception by the official critics. Sergovantzev wrote in the journal *October:* "the social principles of our life, the call to serve the interests of the laboring class, appear as a hostile oppressive force but the Russian righteousness to which Solzhenitsyn alludes appears positive."[7]

One Day in the Life of Ivan Denisovich, "An Incident at Krechetovka Station," and "Matryona's Home" are the best of Solzhenitsyn's works before the appearance of his major books. Is it possible to establish an inner tie among these three works—a path along which the author advanced in his courageous choice of themes and in his aspiration to tell the truth about life? One can probably only guess this path.

One Day in the Life of Ivan Denisovich—unparalleled in literary force, a picture of life behind barbed wire. The cannibalism of the Stalin years! One of its readers, P. R. Martiniuk, writes to the author: "Upon reading this story a question is suggested. How could this happen—the people are in power and yet the people allow such tyranny?" (5: 245).

How could it have happened?

Does not "An Incident at Krechetovka Station" give a partial answer to this question in the depiction of that indispensable "vigilance" that distorts man, that obligatory *party evaluation* of our neighbor and of the occurrences around us? And these notions are certainly not based on commonly accepted standards of spiritual values and morals.

In reflecting upon the battle between good and evil, there are the *počvennicestvo* interpretations of Matryona as a symbol of undying beauty in the folk spirit, scorned and persecuted by the years of a new "troubled times."

It is in this way that many Soviet readers understand this last story,

judging by several letters to *Novyj Mir*. For example: ''I read Matrona
for the fifth time. . . . You [Solzhenitsyn] are yourself that person without whom our country cannot stand. And because of this I have a need
to bow low from the waist, in the Russian fashion, to you for all the
land, for all the Russian people . . .'' (6: 315).

4

Two Choruses:
The First Circle

From here, from this ark, confidently making a path through the darkness, it was easy to survey the winding, straying flow of accursed History.
—*The First Circle*

"Better bread and water than cake and trouble."
—*The First Circle*

1

The First Circle is a book of wide and courageous design. Indeed, in the informative sense it is a virtual "upturning of the virgin soil" of literary silence in the Russia of the Stalinist years—so filled is it with human destinies, problems, revelations, upon which decades of censorship restrictions had been imposed, so relentless is the author's repudiation of evil.

And this, despite the limited scene of action—a small privileged camp on the outskirts of Moscow, which the prisoners call a *sharashka*,[1] and a little bit of Moscow. Also, the time—the entire series of events occurs from the 24th to the 27th of December 1949, so full is Solzhenitsyn's narrative day.

The titles of the eighty-seven chapters of the novel are fascinating and diverse in their associations and style. A title directly referring to the composition of a chapter may alternate with a title containing a key expression or witticism ("A Protestant Christmas," "Boogie-Woogie," "Oh Moment Stay," "Kissing is Forbidden," etc.).

The second chapter of the novel—"Dante's Idea"—explains the title of the book. At the *sharashka* outstanding specialists from various higher fields were gathered from the numerous prison camps. The conditions of living and working were by far better for them. "Perhaps this is a dream? It seems I am in paradise," says one of the newly arrived inmates. "No, dear sir," answers one of the old-timers, "you are still in hell but you have risen to its best and highest circle—the first circle.... The concept of the *sharashka* was conceived, if you will, by Dante—Dante was torn about where to put the ancient wise men.... So Dante thought of a special place for them in hell.'' ''... you are too much of a poet,'' interrupts another prisoner. ''I shall explain to the comrade more simply what a *sharashka* is. One need only read the newspaper article that said, 'It has been proven that a high clip of wool from sheep depends on the animals' feeding and care.' ''

The title itself, referring to Dante's *Inferno*,[2] reveals the general theme of the novel—the punishers and the punished, the triumphant and the oppressed, the chorus of jailers and the chorus of victims.

The presentation of these two choruses in the structure of the novel is polyphonic, as Solzhenitsyn himself would probably call it (in one of his interviews he referred to the polyphonic novel in speaking of his creative work). Each important character, in his role as carrier of a particular theme, is allotted a certain number of chapters,[3] sometimes in succession and sometimes scattered throughout the book, and the voices in both choruses almost resonate together.

The plot that binds the eighty-seven chapters together is not complicated. One of the ''triumphant,'' a government counselor of the second rank, Innokenty Volodin, telephones an old medical professor, who is about to go on a mission to Paris, to warn him that there is danger awaiting him. He had promised to give some information about his work to a French colleague. The MGB knows about this and is preparing an arrest and an ''affair.'' In the telephone booth on the Arbat, Volodin tries to disguise his voice—he is afraid of eavesdroppers. This is the basic intrigue of the plot.

He was right. They had eavesdropped. The next day a recording of his voice is given to the acoustical laboratory of the *sharashka,* where the solution of the problem of voice identification is being attempted. Chapter 82, ''Abandon Hope All Ye Who Enter Here,'' together with the two following chapters describes the procedure of Volodin's arrest and imprisonment in the Lubyanka prison. The promising diplomat becomes a prisoner whose suspenders are removed and whose buttons are cut off.

Innokenty Volodin and his wife Dotnara[4] belong

to that circle of society in which people do not know what it means to walk or take the subway; that group, which even before the war preferred planes to sleeping cars; a group, which never had the headache of furnishing an apartment. Wherever they went—Moscow, Teheran, the Syrian coast, or Switzerland—a furnished dacha, villa, or apartment awaited these young people. Their view was: we have only one life! With such views they were very much in tune with the circumstances in which they lived; and the circumstances were in tune with them. They tried to sample every new and unusual fruit. They learned the taste of every fine cognac, learned to tell the Rhone wines from the Corsican wines and also to recognize all the wines from all the vineyards of the Earth. To wear clothes of every kind, to dance every dance, to swim at every resort. (4: 477)

The daily life and spirit of this "new class" are represented with all their nuances in the scene of the dinner party at Dotnara's father's—the Prosecutor Makarygin (prosecutor of "special cases, that is, cases about which it would not be useful for society to know and which, therefore, were decided upon secretly")—on the occasion of the prosecutor's receiving the second order of Lenin.

In the Makarygins' luxurious apartment, one of the "well-situated" homes, twenty-five guests from the high society of the forties are seated at two tables where "a stately lamp casts multicolored sparkles from its cut crystal facets and ridges." Here is the famous writer-laureate, Galakhov, married to the other Makarygin daughter, Dinera,[5] Major General Slovuta, another very important prosecutor, a certain young man in the government, the reference consultant at the Presidium of the Supreme Soviet, and others. The author's brilliant exposition of these guests— their groupings, movements, arguments, and remarks—is reminiscent of the description of Anna Pavlovna Scherer's soirée, which opens Tolstoy's epic novel. The hostess, according to the tradition of high society, has under her patronage a plain, provincial friend; she is ashamed of her and another guest, Dushan Radovich, in the presence of the important Slovuta--won't he think "that the Makarygins invite riffraff to their home?"

Professor Radovich, an old friend of the prosecutor (true, now he is almost not a friend) is in disfavor—"already in the thirties his lectures were discontinued and his books were not printed." At one time well-known in Comintern circles, he was saving himself from being suppressed now, thanks only to his illnesses. The mind of this unorthodox Marxist is revealed in one small stroke. In Makarygin's study he finds a book written by special request—*Tito, the Traitor's Marshall*. This book, we read in the chapter devoted to Radovich, "The Die-hard," "burned in his lifeless, parchment-like hands.... During the past twelve years thousands and thousands of books had fallen into Radovich's hands—caddish, sycophantic, thoroughly false books—but never, it seemed, had he held such an abomination as this in his hands."

The scene is interesting: Makarygin, Radovich, and Slovuta are in the host's study just before the famous guest leaves for home:

Big-bellied, flesh bulging out from his uniform and overflowing the edge of his high collar, Slovuta surveyed the study with approval.

"You live well, Makarygin! Your elder son-in law has received the Stalin Prize twice?"

"Twice," the prosecutor repeated with satisfaction.

"And the younger is a first counselor?"

"Still second as yet."

"He's a clever boy, and before you know it he'll be an ambassador! And whom are you marrying your youngest daughter to?"

"She's a stubborn girl, Slovuta. I've tried to marry her off but she won't have anything to do with it. She's already waited too long."

"Does that mean she's educated? Looking for an engineer?" When Slovuta laughed his belly shook and his whole body puffed out. "For only eight hundred rubles a month? Marry her off to a Chekist—that's it, marry her off to a Chekist, that's a solid investment! Well, Makarygin, thanks for remembering me; don't keep me any longer, they're waiting and it's almost eleven. And you, Professor, stay healthy. Don't get sick."

"Good-bye, Comrade General."

Radovich got up to shake hands, but Slovuta did not offer his hand to him. (4: 511)

The other world, far more intensive, is presented not in just three, but in most of the chapters of the novel—the *sharashka* world, the world of 280 prisoners locked up in the ark of a special prison, a former church in the village of Mavrino nearby Moscow. Their past is an unreasonable sentence, their future a twenty-five year stretch, their present a four-

walled isolation from outside life. What is left for them? Only the
hidden irony (a parody on Mayakovsky), inaccessible to the investiga-
tions of overseers and jailers.

Moja milicija
Menja sterežet!
V zapretnoj zone
Kak xorošo!
V samom dele—čego nam ešče?... (3: 82)

(My militia guards me! In the forbidden zone, how good it is! Really—
what else do we need?...)

Some of the most impressive scenes of prison life are those meetings
of husband and wife (the chapter called "Kissing is Forbidden" and
chapters 34–38). The straightforwardness and spontaneity of Solzhenitsyn's narrative manner is found here in the very choice of such simple,
and at the same time burning, words to convey the tragedy of the
experiences or situations: "'Larik, my darling,' engineer
Gerasimovich's wife begs him at their meeting, 'Please do something so
you can be freed earlier. You have a brilliant mind. Please invent
something for them. Save me! Save me....' She had not meant to say
that at all. Her heart was broken!... Shaking with sobs and kissing her
husband's small hand, she let her head fall against the rough, warped
little table, which had many of those tears on it" (3: 319).

Or—the Christmas tree which the prisoners were allowed to set up in
a semblance of generosity.

Tomorrow and the day after tomorrow they would set up the Christmas
tree in the semi-circular room. The prisoner-fathers, deprived of their
own children, became children themselves and hung ornaments on it, ...
gathered in a circle, mustached, bearded, and howling the wolf-cry of
their fate, they began to whirl around the tree in bitter laughter:

In the forest was born a pine tree.
In the forest it grew. (4: 797)

More strongly than the cement of plot, the structure of the novel is
bound by the bitter taste of injustice felt by the author who has lived
through a "first circle" of his own. Everywhere the distinct castigation

of cannibalism in whatever form it may be expressed is heard by the reader.

Bitterness and disapproval become transformed into anger, which then engenders satirical nuances in the depiction of jailers of various types and ranks.

The choice of family names is not accidental, for example: "Lieutenant *Zhvakun*[6]—a vulgar wide-mugged impenetrable guy," who served as an executor at military tribunals during the war; also the official critic Zhabov (from *žaba*—"toad"). And linked with the name Zhabov is the description of the writer's "self-scrutiny," which was killing his creative impulse.[7]

The irony hidden in the very tone of the author's exposition is thematically condensed in many of the pages of the novel. In the censure of official anti-American propaganda, for example: "And there was another book on the stool—*American Stories* by some progressive writers . . . the selection was astonishing. Each story was required to have some sort of muck about America. Poisonously gathered together, they presented such a horrible picture that one could only wonder why Americans had not left their country or hung themselves" (3: 235).

Or, from a conversation between the inhabitants of the *sharashka:* " 'When we launch our first flight to the moon, before the countdown, near the rockets, there will of course be a meeting. One of the three members of the crew will be a political indoctrinator,' says an inmate. But another runs up and says, 'Ilya Terentich, I can put you at ease. It won't be that way. . . . The Americans will be the first on the moon ' " (4: 443).

Bitterness and anger establish, also, the satirical inserts of the plot, which are presented somewhat like improvisations. Lovers of literature, or simply "attentive" readers, as Solzhenitsyn would say, cannot overlook Rubin's farce, "The Traitor Prince." So loud is the condemnation of spy-mania and the ominous label "enemy of the people," on the basis of which millions were sent behind barbed wire, that even the stylistic form of parody elicits more of a tragic response than a smile from the reader. ("Rubin jumped off the night table cumbersomely. . . . *Nobody was laughing.*")[8]

More "humorous" is the novella by the engineer Potapov. A famous American woman, transparently identified by the letter R, is shown the humanitarianism of a Soviet prison through a strongly modernized

Potemkin[9] method. "Buddha's Smile." But what a murderous smile! In its sharpness of accusation and mockery this chapter is probably the most vigorous piece of satirical courage in Soviet literature since the twenties. How "shockingly" compressed and complete is, for example, the scene with the priest.

> At this moment, as if by accident, a Russian Orthodox priest entered the cell. He wore a large mother-of-pearl cross on his chest. He was obviously on his regular rounds and was very embarrassed upon finding prison authorities and foreign guests in the cell.
> He wanted to leave, but Mrs. R liked his modesty and asked him to carry on with his duties. The priest then shoved a pocket gospel at one startled prisoner, sat down on a bunk next to another, who was stiff with surprise, and said, "And so my son, last time you asked to be told of the sufferings of Our Lord, Jesus Christ."

And then after the "blessing of the meal," the end of supper, and the entire dramatization, the priest "leaped out of the cell into the midst of the retinue and hurried out before they shut the door" (4: 469–71).

Descriptive and psychological genuineness replace satire in the author's portrayal of the jailers—those at the *sharashka* itself and those in that high "periphery" at whose nod the areas of barbed wire, investigative torture chambers, and prison cells are maintained and multiplied.

At the *sharashka* there is the moon-faced, gently smiling junior lieutenant of the MGB, Nadelashin, who, after having watched and listened, wrote everything down in a tattletale's notebook from which he reported to his superiors. Majors Myshin and Shikin represent the spirit of police vigilance and investigation in the special prison: "what a vile, gray-haired louse—his hair grayed over the analysis of denunciations—is this Major Shikin. How idiotically minute is his knowledge, what a lot of cretinism is found in all of his suggestions," thinks one of the *sharashka* chiefs, Yakonov (4: 631).

Then there is the memorable character of the minister of state security, Abakumov. It is more than just with irony, rather it is with the accuracy of observation and evaluation that the description of the police's characteristics in the execution of duty is drawn: "from a long lack of exercise the minister's mind had become useless to him. Through his entire career he had lost out whenever he tried to think and won out with a demonstration of official zeal. Abakumov tried to strain his head as little as possible'' (3: 109).

The ears constitute (in the Tolstoyan tradition) a leitmotif of Abakumov's portrait. Out of fear they ''at first grew ice cold, then they let off and began to burn—and each time Abakumov grew even more afraid, so that his persistently burning ears would arouse the Boss's suspicion.'' In Stalin's office ''he stood, with his long arms at his side, leaning slightly forward with a respectful smile of greeting on his meaty lips— and his ears were aflame.'' They cooled down only after a satisfactory conclusion of the night conversation.

This conversation between the dictator and his minister of security, for all who are acquainted with the circumstances of the forties, sounds like a veritable whispering of history itself.

> With his head still turned up like a crow with a wrung neck, Stalin watched him attentively.
> ''Listen,'' he asked still in thought, ''what about it? Are there still acts of terrorism? They haven't stopped?''
> Abakumov sighed bitterly. ''I would be glad to tell you, Iosif Vissarionovich, that there are no cases of terrorism. But there are. We find them even in stinking kitchens, even in the marketplace.''
> Stalin closed one eye and satisfaction was visible in the other. ''That's good,'' he nodded. ''That means you are working.'' (3: 153–154)

The image of Stalin is undoubtedly one of the pinnacles of Solzhenitsyn's creation. ''Here,'' Lukacs writes in his book on Solzhenitsyn, ''Solzhenitsyn showed himself to be a penetrating and great artist.'' One can only guess what sources of information concerning the inaccessible Kremlin ruler led to the creation of this image. Where, for example, was the genuineness of Stalin's speech mannerisms and intonation drawn from? Was he assisted in this way by stories from Stalin's former war buddies who later found themselves in prison camps?[10] By the study of written materials—articles by Stalin, speeches and interviews?[11] Or was there, above and beyond all this, an artistic intuition that instilled the breath of life into such lines as, for example: ''He was just a plain old man with a dried-up double chin (it was never shown in portraits), a mouth permeated with the smell of Turkish leaf tobacco and fat fingers which left their traces on books. He had not been feeling well yesterday and today. Even in the warm air he felt a chill on his back and shoulders, and so he covered them with a brown camelhair shawl'' (3: 122–123).

2

Among the chorus of victims at the center of the author's attention are the figures of prisoners working in two laboratories—"the acoustical" and "number seven"—by Stalin's order to produce a secret telephone. These are the mathematician Gleb Nerzhin, the philologist Rubin, the engineers Sologdin, Pryanchikov, Bobynin, Gerasimovich, and others.

Nerzhin's character is autobiographical. His profession, his interest in linguistics, his writing (on "little pieces of paper" hidden in the desk), and his past correspond with that of the author. Here is a comparison of several features of Nerzhin's biography with Solzhenitsyn's autobiography.

Novel:
... the war began, and Nerzhin at first found himself a driver in the transport corps, and weighted down with resentment. Clumsily he chased the horses to pasture. . . .

Then Nerzhin made his way up to artillery officer. He again became youthful and capable. He went around in a tight fitting belt. . . .

Then Nerzhin was arrested. (4: 541–542)

Autobiography:
... at the beginning [of the war] because of poor health, I became a driver in the transport corps, and I spent the winter of 1941–42 there. Then only, thanks again to mathematics, I was transferred to artillery school. . . . I was made a commander of an artillery reconnaissance battery.

I was arrested. . . . (*Grani* no. 80, p. 5)

The tragedy of the broken family and the gloominess to which the prisoners' dear ones were doomed is also taken from the fate of the author himself. Creatively, this is the warmest element in Nerzhin's profile. His wife Nadya is included in the greater plan of the novel, which is almost presented as "theme within theme" and step by step. Thus she draws gradually closer to the reader.

We see her in passing on the subway, begging MGB Lieutenant Colonel Klimentiev, whom she has met by accident, for a meeting with her husband. We see her more closely in the chapter "Be

Unfaithful''—in scenes from the past (when for the first time she was not paid her allocation as an officer's wife; when a tattered triangle of paper had arrived—"My dearest! Now it will be another ten years!''). Even more closely we see Nadya at her meeting with Nerzhin, mostly through the eyes of her husband—the constraint of movements and words under the eye of the bulldog overseer, the snatches of remarks and glances ("You're thin," he said sympathetically. "You should eat better. Can't you eat better?" "Am I homely?" her look asked. "You're just as wonderful as ever!" her husband's glance replied).

Finally Nadya's inner character is fully revealed in the student dormitory (chapters 44–47), where she is forced to hide her lot from her friends. It is revealed with that special attention to details, situations, and features with a significance that in Solzhenitsyn borders on the intensity of symbol.[12] Such is the final scene of the chapter "The Resurrection of the Dead''—Nadya has rejected the courting of Shchagov, having disclosed to him that her husband is a prisoner. He leaves, as it seems to her, frightened by this revelation. In the music being played in the adjoining room, her own desperation is heard.

> Leaning her forehead against the middle pane, Nadya touched the other cold panes with outstretched hands.
>
> She stood like someone crucified on the black crossbeams of the window.
>
> There had been a tiny, tiny warm spot in her life, and it was gone.
>
> . . .
>
> Nadya had forgotten all about Schagov, when he came back in without knocking.
>
> He carried two small glasses with a bottle.
>
> "Well, soldier's wife," he said cheerfully and coarsely. "Don't lose heart! Take a glass. If you keep your wits, you will be happy. Let's drink to the resurrection of the dead!" (3: 408)

After the meeting with his wife Nerzhin breaks off the relationship that had begun to take shape between himself and Simochka, an employee for "surveillance" with the rank of lieutenant in the MGB. "I would consider myself a scoundrel if I didn't confess to you," he says to her. "Yesterday . . . I saw my wife."

Sometimes the female characters in the novel are, to a certain degree, subsidiary; they underline motifs that are more important for the author.

Such is the case with Simochka. Before her assignment to the special prison she had received a lengthy instruction by the MGB about the sort of "snakepit" she would fall into and the cunning and dangerous prisoners she would meet. But after a month of work, she could not discern in these people anything criminal. They—we read in the novel— "awakened only unqualified respect in her, for their varied knowledge and their steadfastness in bearing difficulties." Required to report to the prison authorities about the actions and words of those individuals under her surveillance, she falls in love with one of them.

Nerzhin's character is autobiographical not only because of his "service record" but because of his attitude—above all, his irreconcilability toward that which threw him and many others like him into prison—an uncompromising steadfastness, courageous and sacrificing.

The culmination of Nerzhin's inner state of mind is contained in a scene from the first day of *sharashka* life described by the author. The chief of the decoding project, Colonel of Engineers Yakanov, proposes that Nerzhin transfer to "number seven" closer to the "tentacles of cryptography," where there would no longer be any time for reflection and his secret "little pieces of paper."

"If the work is successful, as a cryptographer you will be freed ahead of time; the conviction will be removed from your record, and you will be given an apartment in Moscow, . . ." he is told by Verenyov, an old assistant professor of mathematics in Yakonov's office.

"They will remove the conviction from my record!" Nerzhin cries angrily, his eyes narrowing. "Where did it occur to you that I want that little gift—you did a good job so we'll free you, forgive you—. . . . Let them admit first that one shouldn't put people in prison for their ways of thinking, and then *we* will see whether we will forgive *them*" (3: 63).

The rejection of this proposal means that he will be sent back to a general camp. At the *sharashka* he can have his fill of work that can be done without freezing his hands off. "All the arguments of reason— yes, I agree, Citizen Chief! All the arguments of the heart—get thee hence, Satan!"

And hearing this rejection, Yakonov notes down—"Nerzhin to be *sent away.*"

This steadfastness—as the conscience of humanity, as the persistent demand for justice—is shown by many other *sharashka* prisoners, oppressed and deprived of their civil rights, fearless and strong in their inner spiritual freedom. "You need me but I don't need you," Engineer Bobynin hurls into the face of Abakumov. "A person from whom you have taken *everything* is no longer in your power. He is free all over again."

Another engineer, Gerasimovich (whose ears still ring with his wife's plea at their meeting, "Please invent something. Save me! Save me!") refuses to build a special "spy" camera ("which at night would take a picture of a person and whoever he is with on the street, and he would never know as long as he lived..."). He refuses even though the success of the project would mean his freedom. "No! That's not my specialty! Putting people in prison is not my specialty!" he says (4: 696).

Nerzhin and also Rubin and Sologdin are intellectual heroes, in the sense that they are able to think even "against the current." Skepticism, happiness, people, and personality. Is each historical development in order? Can we justify terror? Do the wheels of history really roll on inevitably toward Communism? These are the problems that trouble them, and in this respect they are pioneers among their contemporary literary heroes, whose authors did not dare allow an expression of independent thought.

Nerzhin's *narodničestvo*[13] is original because it includes a denial of that tinsel idol created by the literature of the last century, and an affirmation of his own disillusionment and searching. Having understood that "the people have no homespun superiority to him," Nerzhin comes to the conclusion that "the people" are grouped together, "not by birth, not by physical labor, not by the wings of education, but by spirit." Each of us must "cut and polish one's soul so as to become a *person*" (4: 544).

The Tolstoyanism of this concept is continued in the chapter called "Going to the People" with its image of Spiridon, the janitor. It seems to Nerzhin that Spiridon is an example of such a soul, a soul of folk strength and configuration. This character, richly sculpted with splendid language (Spiridon's dream alone—in "Monday Dawn"—in which he sees his beloved pink mare Grivna!), is often compared with Tolstoy's Platon Karataev by some critics. Beyond Spiridon's stability, integrity, and fairness, it seems to Nerzhin that there is also a mysterious, philosophical folk wisdom in him: "Didn't this [Spiridon's actions] somehow tally with the Tolstoyan doctrine that in the world there are no innocent and no guilty individuals?... Didn't these almost instinctive actions of a red-headed peasant comprise a world system of philosophical skepticism?'' (4: 558).

The correlation with Tolstoy appears in the final episode of the Spiridon theme, when Nerzhin asks the janitor about innocence and guilt and the latter answers with a resounding aphorism, which Nerzhin takes as a kind of revelation. *Anna Karenina* immediately comes to mind here and especially the conversation between Levin and the peasant, Fyodor, about the God-fearing old man, Fokanych. This conversation serves as the final ray of illumination in the hero's quest. The closeness of both episodes is not only thematic but also structural and stylistic.

The First Circle	*Anna Karenina*
"... Is it conceivable that any human being on earth can determine who is right and who is wrong? Who can be sure of that?"	"Why will he [give credit]?"
"Well, I will tell you," an animated Spiridon replied readily... "I will tell you: the wolfhound is right and the cannibal is wrong."	"Well it's this way. It seems that there are many different types of people. Take Mityukha, he lives only to satisfy his needs. But Fokanych is a righteous old man. He lives for his soul. He remembers God."
"What? What?" said Nerzhin, overwhelmed by the simplicity and force of the answer. (4: 561)	"What do you mean remembers God? What do you mean lives only for his soul?" Levin almost shouted.
	. . .
	"Yes, yes. Good-bye!" stammered Levin, panting with agitation... ⋅

The closeness is not eclipsed by the difference between the questions themselves. Levin's ethical-religious problem of "how to live" becomes concentrated in Nerzhin's case into the problem of how to conduct oneself under the conditions of all-penetrating violence in society. Does one keep aloof or does one interfere, in turn resorting to violence? Nerzhin's question is sociological and is evidently tied in with his argument with Rubin the night before. It concerns the justification of government constraint, a government which by its very nature is itself a form of constraint. But Rubin contended that "the state cannot exist without a well organized penal system,'' and this seemed unacceptable to Nerzhin. Spiridon's answer perhaps surprised him with its admission of government inherent in the first part of the aphorism (''the wolfhound is right''); but Nerzhin could not doubt Spiridon's condemnation of cannibalism.

In his arguments with Rubin, essentially the same problem is resolved in the scheme of the philosophy of history. Rubin affirms the conformity of the historical development to the law, and in particular the timeliness and greatness of Stalin. ''He is the greatest of men! Someday you will understand he is at the same time the Robespierre and the Napoleon of our Revolution.'' ''Historians no longer concern themselves with history,'' Nerzhin returns, emphasizing the doubtlessness of such a conclusion under the conditions of nonfreedom and the requirements of singing hymns to Stalin. ''I see who wins the prizes and who is paid the academic salaries. They don't write history; they just lick a certain well-known spot.''

The justification of any means if it leads to the desired end is the subject of Rubin's argument with Sologdin. *''The higher the ends, the higher the means should be.* Treacherous means in themselves destroy the end itself,'' states Sologdin. The argument switches to the personal moral steadfastness of the debaters and reaches a culmination when Rubin expresses his doubts about Sologdin's steadfastness: ''Plainly you don't have the talent to distinguish yourself. . . . If they call you, you will crawl on your belly.''

The image of the young and talented engineer, Sologdin, is elaborated in the light of Rubin's very conviction, that is, in the light of a collision between the creative personality and totalitarianism, a collision which so often ends in compromise.

This theme is revealed in the scene of Sologdin's ''duel'' with Colonel of Engineers Yakonov (''Two Engineers''), a scene of powerful and artistic prose. Sologdin has burned a sketch of an absolute encoder he had designed, not wanting to risk the possibility that his invention would be appropriated by the local chiefs, who would then have the inventor himself sent away on a transport:

> Between the two engineers no further questions or explanations were needed. A current of insane frequency and unendurable tension passed through their locked stares.

"I will destroy you!" declared the eyes of the colonel.

"Collar me for a third term, you bastard!" screamed the prisoner's eyes. (4: 637)

But the fervor of the designer-inventor, his urge to contrast his jailer's helplessness with his own knowledge and talent, wins out. Sologdin agrees to reconstruct the design and to complete the construction in a month's time needed by Yakonov. He does not have the strength for Nerzhin's "Get thee hence, Satan!"

How do we resolve the thematic image of Rubin? Rubin has a dual nature. He is a party member, who continues to be true to it and to justify Stalin's terror even in prison; at the same time he improvises the brilliant antigovernment farces about "The Traitor Prince"; a defender of the dogmatic dialectical materialism, he is at the same time a dreamer (is not Rubin somewhat of a Rudin of Turgenev's novel?), and with complete originality he jogs the problem of human happiness found in the second part of Goethe's *Faust*. In his duel of words with Nerzhin and Sologdin he emerges neither as victor nor as one completely defeated.

That which demolishes him as a defender of party dictatorship is something else. At night after a cruel skirmish with Sologdin, he develops a throbbing ache near his liver. Walking through the foul corridors, in vain expectation of the doctor's assistant, suffocating with pain, Rubin turns his thoughts to the past. Some time ago when he was still a youth "anxious to prove his usefulness both to himself and to the one revolutionary class," Rubin with a Mauser in his hand had gone off to collectivize a village. Memories, themselves painful—the voice of conscience—which he had no desire to awaken ("to forget them meant to be healed"), overpower him. His character is suddenly illuminated for the reader with a whole new light. Here is an excerpt:

It all seemed perfectly natural—to dig up pits filled with buried grain, to stop the owners from milling their flour and baking bread, to prevent them from drawing water from the well. If a peasant child died—drop dead, you devil, and your children with you, but you won't bake bread. It produced no pity in him but became as usual like a city streetcar, that

solitary cart drawn by an exhausted horse, going through a stifled village besieged with death. A knock of the whip at the shutters: "Any
corpses? Bring them out."

. . .

But now he felt a burning pressure in his head, as if he were seared
with a redhot brand. And sometimes it seemed as if his wounds were for
that! Prison was for that! His sickness was for that!

Therefore his imprisonment was just. But if he understood now that
what he had done had been terrible, that he would never repeat such
actions, that they had been atoned for . . . how could he cleanse himself
of it? To whom could he say that it had never taken place. From now on
let's consider that it had never taken place. We shall act as if it had
never happened! (4: 579)

3

Rubin's terrible night is only the continuation of a theme that actually
opens the novel—the awakening of conscience. Innokenty Volodin's
act of warning Professor Dobroumov, an old acquaintance of his family,
about the MGB's intended provocation is not just an accidental impulse,
but the final link for a continuous process. The preceding links were
satiated with "all the fruits of the earth that could be smelled, felt, eaten
or squeezed," and his reflections upon his mother's diaries and letters,
in which he read and reread something that had long been forgotten,
suddenly seemed to carry an illumination: "Pity is the first act of a good
soul. What is the most precious thing in the world? To know that you
have not participated in injustices. They are stronger than you. They
have been and will be, but let them come about not through you" (4:
481).

Thus the "enlightened" Volodin (not only life but conscience is
given to you only once) in his conversation with his brother-in-law,
Galakhov, speaks about the lack of conscience in the thick journals and
defines the writer's tragedy in a formula that has probably been insured
literary immortality: "a great writer . . . is like a country's second government. Therefore no regime has ever loved its great writers, only its
minor ones" (4: 503).

And so Volodin, enlightened by an awakening of conscience, while
hesitating to enter the telephone booth, pronounces another aphorism,
which should have been stamped into the memo pads and primers of his

contemporaries. "If one is forever cautious, can one remain a human being?"[14]

Volodin not only knows but seems to have a presentiment about the consequences of his step. The place prepared for him at the end of the novel is described with a figurative, almost symbolic, periphrasis:

> He sensed a new meaning in the new building of the Bolshaya Lubyanka which faced Furkasovsky Lane. This nine-storied, grey-black hulk was a battleship, and the eighteen pilasters hung on its starboard side like eighteen gun turrets.[15] A solitary and frail canoe, Innokenty was drawn toward it, across a little square, under the prow of a heavy swift ship.
>
> He turned away, to save himself. . . . (3: 8)

Yet nevertheless, "Listen to me, listen!" he yells into the receiver, to the professor's wife, who does not want to hear him out as she should. "He must not give the foreigners anything! It could be used as a pro-voca. . . ."

Someone had broken the connection (3: 10).

There is yet another "awakening" in this "triumphant chorus"— Clara, the daughter of Prosecutor Makarygin. Here the process is actually only suggested. The beginning: a poorly dressed woman is washing the staircase in the house where the prosecutor's family is getting a new apartment. The women looks up at Clara and her mother as they pass by. She raises her intelligent face splashed with dirty water, at the rustling of their silk dresses, at the smell of their perfume, a face Clara is unable to forget.

Subsequently, Clara undergoes an experience that is common to other women working at the *sharashka*. She recognizes the real substance "of those monsters in overalls" and she raises questions, unseemly from the lips of the special prosecutor's daughter. Why? What for? How can this be: "they do what they want?"

Such is one of the main inner themes of the novel—the theme of the awakening of conscience.

Alongside this theme is the no less significant inner theme of the novel, which arises more or less distinctly in several unrelated places. It is difficult to give this theme a special definition. Each reader may interpret it in his own way. One could call it the theme of turning to Heaven as to a force that can resist the militant nonspirituality in the materialistic world view.

"A human being is instilled with a certain essence at birth," the old artist, Kondrashev-Ivanov, tells Nerzhin. "It is, as it were, the nucleus of the person. It is his 'I'. And it is still unknown which forms which—whether life forms the man or man with his strong spirit forms his life. Because . . . he has something to measure up to, somewhere he can *turn to*. Because in him is the image of perfection which in rare moments suddenly emerges before his spiritual gaze" (3: 359).

That which specifically emerges before his spiritual gaze cannot be named here; it is only allegorically alluded to. Furthermore, this allegory is repeated in the language of colors. The artist shows Nerzhin a sketch of his life's work—above a mountain gorge is a rider. Perplexed and amazed, he looks into the distance "where a reddish-gold radiance flooded the whole upper vault of the sky" and "vague yet visible in its unearthly perfection stood the violet aureate castle of the Holy Grail" (3: 360–361).

An even fuller and more richly artistic presentation of the theme of turning to Heaven appears in the chapter "The Church of St. John the Baptist." Colonel of Engineers Yakonov, after a crushing dressing down by Abakumov concerning his responsibility for the secret telephone, confusedly dismisses his chauffeur. Not knowing where he is going, he begins to walk. His feet bring him to the banks of the Yauza, a tributary of the Moscow River, to some ruins that strangely and sharply remind him of his past. He was twenty-six years old then, and Agniya, the girl whom he had loved, was twenty-one. "Would you like me to show you one of the most beautiful places in Moscow?" she asked. And she showed him this small, brick church of St. John the Baptist with a tent-shaped belltower, all beautifully inserted into the landscape of autumn leaves, the river shining in the sun, and the city.

The majesty of this display, its own "foreshortening," contains an inner parallel to what Nerzhin had seen in Kondrashev's picture of "The Castle of the Holy Grail"—both are an emancipation from the earth-bound feeling, a turning toward perfection, beauty, and eternity.

The church has been destroyed. Coming out of his memories,

Yakonov peers into the ruins, and he is imbued with the smell of decay and dampness issuing from it. He stands for a long time leaning on the stone embrasure of the rusty door. And further:

> Yakonov was at the peak of his visible power. He held a high rank in a powerful ministry. He was smart, talented—and reputed to be smart and talented. His loving wife waited for him at home. His rosy-cheeked children slept in their little beds. He had an excellent apartment with high-ceilinged rooms and a balcony in an old Moscow building. His monthly salary was measured in the thousands. A personal Pobeda awaited his call. Yet he stood there with his elbows leaning against dead stones, and he did not want to live any longer. (3: 182–183)

The chapter is interesting because of the significance (deeper meaning) that so often brings Solzhenitsyn's prose to the border of symbol. Some readers would, without a doubt, see it as a symbol, perhaps even as the central one in the novel—the symbol of the tragic loss of faith and love, a loss that can only lead the human soul to numbness and disintegration.

The lyricism with which the entire chapter, the most poetic in the novel, is narrated includes many components in the artistic structure. In *The First Circle* the very rare landscape description is concise and, as a rule, is more or less a distant setting (for example, the winter morning at the *sharashka*): "The day was just beginning to break. Obscured by snowy clouds, the sky was late with its morning glow. The lamps still cast yellow circles on the snow" (4: 600).

But the landscape that Agniya and Anton Yakonov see in "The Church of St. John the Baptist" seems to be a prolongation of their inner gaze, as if dissolving themselves within themselves:

> Anton drew in his breath. It was as if they had suddenly been torn out of the crowded city and had come out on a height with a broad open view into the distance. The church portico at the main entrance stretched through a break in the parapet into a long white stairway which had many flights and landings down the hillside to the Moscow River. The river burned in the sun. On the left lay the Zamoskvorechye, casting blinding yellow reflections from its windows, and below, the black chimneys of the Moscow Electrica Power Plant belched smoke into the sunset sky;

the gleaming Yauza flowed almost under one's feet into the Moscow River; beyond it to the right stretched the Foundling Home; and behind it rose the carved contours of the Kremlin. Still farther off, the five gilded cupolas of the Cathedral of Christ the Saviour flamed in the sun.

And in all this golden radiance Agniya, with a yellow shawl thrown around her shoulders seemed golden too as she sat squinting at the sun. . . . "Yes, that's Moscow!" said Anton with emotion. (3: 176)

The same applies to character portrayal. Usually in the traditional form of description (for example, the portrait of Nerzhin), it is sometimes limited to an emphasis upon certain separate features (Spiridon is "redheaded, with a round face, his immobile eyes looked ill under his thick reddish eyebrows"; Rubin has eyes that are "big and warm" and he often "plucks at the strands of his coarse wiry black beard with one hand").

But there is Agniya, fashioned in a different manner, a lyrically abstract manner, slightly reminiscent of Pasternak: "The girl was not of this world. It was her misfortune to be refined and demanding beyond that point where it was possible to live. Her brows and nostrils sometimes quivered like wings when she spoke, as if she were getting ready to fly away . . ." (3: 172–173).

And the *words* themselves included in this chapter of images are lyrical and a bit illusory:

> He uttered her name aloud—Agniya—and, like a soft wind, completely different, forgotten sensations stirred in that body that had been so sated by the good things in life. (3: 172)

> The transparent yellow shawl slid down over her shoulders and rested on her free, half-lowered elbows like a pair of golden wings. (3: 179)

> Agniya said in her soft, *woodsy* voice. . . . (3: 175)

The First Circle is a ruthless rejection of Stalinism.

In 1964 *Novyj Mir* made an agreement with Solzhenitsyn to publish his book. Was it wiser never to make this agreement a reality?

The title—*The First Circle*—has to do not only with what goes on behind prison walls, but it has to do with an even broader phenomenon, which it embraces.

And, whether or not by symbolic accident (probably, by no means the author's intention), if one were to take the initial letters of the title in Russian (*V K*ruge *P*ervom), the result would be VKP (*V*sesojuznaja *K*ommunisticeskaja *P*artija—the Communist Party of the Soviet Union)!

5

Kostoglotov—Rusanov: *Cancer Ward*

My God, it's about time! It's long overdue. How could it be otherwise? A man is dying from a tumor—how can a country live sprouting concentration camps and exiles?

—*Cancer Ward*

1

Solzhenitsyn writes in his *Autobiography:* "With a month's respite after an eight-year term without a new sentence and even without an 'OSO[1] decree', an administrative order was issued not to free me but to send me to perpetual exile in Kok-Terek (South Kazakhstan). . . . There I quickly developed cancer. At the end of 1953, deprived of the ability to eat or sleep and poisoned by the tumorous venom, I was already on the verge of death. I was allowed to go for medical treatment at Tashkent and was cured at the cancer clinic there in 1954 (*Cancer Ward,* "The Right Hand"). . . ."

Cancer Ward is the most "monolithic" of Solzhenitsyn's works, probably because of its strong autobiographical elements, its composition, and its artistic expressiveness.

The narrative space is almost completely limited to one ward with nine beds, and its concentration is on the fates and experiences of a few patients; the "vertical," temporal axis of the plot is the story of one man's convalescence.

The recovering Oleg Kostoglotov is the autobiographical hero of the novel. His spiritual world is revealed more openly to us than that of Nerzhin in *The First Circle.* The pulse of life is fuller. Perhaps because it is a pulse doomed to die and one is forced to follow its throbbing with Kostoglotov all the time.

Like Nerzhin, Kostoglotov is a lover of truth. But at the same time he is more lyrical; his words are not only about justice but also about love—love for women, the dear earth, the sky, the trees. There is quite a bit of nature description in the book and that lyrical expression which gives the narrative material such artistic persuasiveness.

Most important of all, everything or nearly everything in the novel is seen through Kostoglotov's own eyes and is presented in his terms, which the author himself adopts. It is seen with that special tenacity and sharpness with which, according to many witnesses, people grasp features and details as they approach or face death.

All in all, *Cancer Ward* is a creative achievement of the first order. "The novel gives a stunning impression—a work of unusual artistic power," commented G. Berezko at a discussion on the book at the Moscow Writers' Association on 16 November 1966 (6: 187).

The reader together with Pavel Nikolayevich Rusanov goes up into the lobby and sees the dirty dressing gowns of the patients, smells the "moisture-filled, oppressive, peculiarly medicinal" air that reeks from behind the doors of the ward, and hears the cold-blooded remark by a stocky patient with a tightly bandaged neck—"Another nice little cancer."

Later, at the above-mentioned discussion of his work, Solzhenitsyn states: "Actually the entrance of Rusanov into the ward is autobiographical; it is I myself who steps over the threshold of the cancer ward" (6: 185–186).

This "I myself" explains the inner "pulsation" of the novel, what we usually call its creative power and genuineness. The author lived through the row of destinies on the hospital beds with all the circumstances of torment and human despair before oncoming death or the scalpel.

Also part of his experience are the treatments and doctors. Vivid portrayals of doctors emerge. Probably an image unique in its creative vitality not only for postrevolutionary Soviet literature is that of Ludmila Afanasyevna Dontsova, the director of the Radiation Division in the clinic. More than sixty pages are devoted to her story. Having been exposed during her years of work to x-rays of more destructive doses "than the most enduring and seriously ill patients," hers is a story of undeclared but unfeigned righteousness and activity in spirit and work.

Often Solzhenitsyn in a very short passage—one or two remarks or an exchange of glances—reveals the inner spirit of a character. Already stricken with the same illness she has cured others of, Dontsova makes her final rounds. She stops at the bed of Sigbatov who is hopelessly ill:

> "You see, Sharaf," said Dontsova's eyes, "I did what I could. But
> I'm wounded and I'll soon be falling too."
> "I know that," the Tartar's eyes answered. "The one who gave birth
> to me, couldn't have done more for me. But now here I am. I can do
> nothing to save you." (2: 500)

The profiles of patients, the scenes of their spiritual confusion and
anguish are real experiences too. Sigbatov, "the most gentle and most
courteous man in the clinic," can no longer hold his sacrum straight,
"and only two strong hands pressed against his back maintained his
verticality." The tractor driver Proshka "in order to accelerate the
turnover of bedspace" is discharged with the diagnosis *tumor cordis*—a
cancerous tumor on the heart. Happy that he is being released, he waves
cheerfully to the rest of the patients and leaves only to die at home.
There are the young people—sixteen-year-old Dyomka and Asya ("a
blonde-haired, pining angel, untouchable"). A love affair could have
developed between them but Dyomka is flat on his back with an amputated leg, and Asya comes running up to him in tears—they have to cut
off her breast.

This is one of those unforgettable scenes. "You are the last one!"
says Asya to Dyomka. "The last one who can still see it and kiss it."
And he kisses her "doomed right one." "You will remember, won't
you? . . . You'll remember it was there and what it was like?" Asya's
tears dropped onto his close-cropped head (2: 439).

The young geologist Vadim does not want to use pull "even in the
horrible face of cancerous death." Then there is the meek Federau and
the richly drawn, roguish provision supplier, Maxim Chaly, the only
character or one of the few handled with a humorous touch. Yefrem
Podduyev is stricken with cancer of the tongue.

The image of Yefrem Podduyev is one of greatness and depth. He is
very much "of the soil." Perhaps, this is why the phraseology in
sections dealing with him have a folkish word choice and an almost
skaz-like intonation. A section in translation reads:

> Yefrem's tongue was sore—his quick, well-formed, inconspicuous
> tongue. He had never really paid attention to it, but it was always so
> useful to him in life. In fifty years he had given this tongue a lot of

exercise. With it he had talked his way into a salary he had never earned, sworn that he had done things he hadn't, laid himself out for things he didn't believe in. He had shouted at bosses and insulted workers. With it he piled filth on all that was dear and holy, delighting in his trills like a nightingale. He told fat-assed stories, but never touched politics. He sang Volga songs. He lied to many women all over the place that he wasn't married, that he had no children, that he'd be back in a week and then they would start building a home. (2: 112)[2]

Yefrem continues the theme of conscience, which so fully reverberated through *The First Circle*. Dying, he is tormented by the memory of the women he has deceived. ("It was hard to imagine how many women Yefrem had gone through.") And there is another memory—of an apparently insignificant and distant event. As a foreman over convicts who were constructing a gas main, Yefrem refused to make allowances for three prisoners completely worn out from shoveling. "All right, chief. It'll be your turn to die someday," said one of them looking up from the pit. And when the patients in the ward discuss the possibility of healing by self-hypnosis, Yefrem wheezes hopelessly, "For that one probably needs . . . a clean conscience."

Yefrem's spiritual confusion is, however, even more complex. He has read Tolstoy's story "What Men Live By" in a book Kostoglotov gave him. The problem of Christian love, which he has simply passed up for lack of time in the pursuit "of bread alone," now becomes for him the problem of his life's meaning. Perhaps with it, with love, one should meet death?

Yefrem asks those in the ward the question "What do men live by?" He does not receive a satisfactory answer.

But this Tolstoyan question of his forms the most important structural axis of the novel. The axis of its inner conflict—Kostoglotov vs. Rusanov.

2

Kostoglotov exemplifies the fighting spirit of nonconformity, truth, and love of life. The ruggedness and straightforwardness of his soul are excellently presented. He is a man who "would love to break through those thick skulls and demonstrate justice," who "never allowed himself to smile at his jailers even if they smiled at him," who, even in conversation with a well-intentioned doctor, "looked unappeasable, like a black hound." Finally, he took no pains to avoid coarseness in his language.

This somewhat callous image grows warmer on pages where the memories of his first night out of prison are related ("Take Up Thy Bed and Walk"), or where Kostoglotov's romantic love for Vera Gangart is presented, and especially in the story of his unexpected return to life.

Vera Gangart ("Vega"), the most poetic character in the novel, sets the stifled "nonviolent" strings of Kostoglotov's soul vibrating again: "he knew that this woman, this gentle almost ethereal creature, moving softly and thinking about every move, would not make the slightest mistake" ("Transfusion of Blood").

As Vera Gangart listens to a suite from the "Sleeping Beauty" at home, she imagines how Kostoglotov, drenched from the rain and doomed for death, would listen to this suite (he had tried to get to the theater while he was in the city). Then she has an imaginary conversation with him as if he were sitting across from her:

> She was developing her theory about men and women. Hemingway's supermen were beings who had not yet raised themselves to a human level. Hemingway swam in shallow water. . . . That is not really what a woman needs from a man. What she needs is attentive tenderness and a sense of security from him. He should be her shield and her shelter. (And it was with Oleg, a man without rights, deprived of all significance as a citizen, that Vega for some reason had this feeling of being protected.)
>
> And his notions about women were even more confused. Carmen was thought to be the most feminine of women. The most feminine woman was declared to be the one who most actively searched for pleasure. But that is a pseudo-woman, a man dressed in women's clothes." (2: 381–382)

The actual story of Kostoglotov's recovery is noted in two lyrical sections:

First, the interior monologue that concludes the eleventh chapter, in which the ordinary but invaluable human rights discovered by Kostoglotov upon his recovery are listed: "the right to move about without waiting for an order; the right to be alone; the right to look at the stars without being blinded by prison searchlights; the right to shut the light at night and sleep in the dark; the right to drop a letter in the mailbox; the right to rest on Sunday; the right to go swimming in the river. Yes, there were many more such rights. And among them was the right to talk with women'' (2; 174).

Finally—the last two chapters, in which Kostoglotov's departure from the cancer clinic turns into an unexpected, rediscovered future, contain some very lyrical lines.

But Kostoglotov's actual world view is revealed only in his conflict with Rusanov. The theme of the two men forms a kind of compositional circle beginning with the very first pages of the novel. Upon entering the ward, Rusanov's first look at Kostoglotov is filled with a kind of hatred toward this ''cutthroat'' who ''had pretentions to culture—he had almost finished reading a book.'' Thus we are given an adverse picture of Kostoglotov through Rusanov's eyes.

The circle closes with the scene of their last meeting. Lavrik, Rusanov's son (named in honor of Lavrenty Beria), has come to bring his father home. As they leave the hospital, their car almost runs down Kostoglotov, who is walking across the street.

> ''I called him Bone-chewer. If you only knew what an unpleasant, envious type he is,'' said Rusanov to his wife... ''A class enemy....''
> ''I should have run him down. Why did you tell me to honk?'' laughed Lavrik.
>
> . . .
>
> But Kostoglotov flung a long string of obscenities after them, carrying on to his heart's content. (2: 512–513)

Rusanov to some degree is a Chekhovian ''Man in a Case,'' but in a new, postrevolutionary setting with a volume of party dogma and behavior under his arm. He has the same vigilance and tendency to denounce as Chekhov's Belikov except that he is in the service of a contemporary established authority. Belikov was unwaveringly convinced of the grandeur of the classical Greek language. He would raise his finger and say with great profundity—''Antropos!'' Just as convinced, Rusanov feasts on his pieces of chicken and answers Yefrem Podduyev's question ''What do men live by?'' ''There is no doubt about the answer. Remember. Men live by their ideological principles and the interests of their society.''

Rusanov himself directs his denunciations and betrayals with an ideological conscience; he must do his duty. Rodichev, a former neighbor and friend; press operator Grusha, imprisoned for some talk against the Leader of the People; her daughter who drowned herself after Rusanov threatened to bring her up on charges of improprieties in her forms; the engineer of bourgeois education, Edward Christoforovich, who at one time had called Rusanov a fool in front of everybody; and so many more were all ruined by him! "In that excellent and honorable time—1937 and 1938," he thinks, "the social atmosphere was noticeably cleansed and it became so easy to breathe! All the liars and slanderers, those who had been too apt in their self criticism, those very slick intellectuals all disappeared or shut up or hid, while the people of principle, the steady, loyal, friends of Rusanov and he himself walked with their deserving heads held high" (2: 215).

And therefore: "What right do they have to release them? How can people be so mercilessly traumatized?"

He is supported in this monstrous indifference to the victims by a member of his family with similar views: "Well, all right, they were convicted rightly or wrongly a long time ago and sent away into exile—but why bring them back now? . . . And what does the very word 'rehabilitated' mean. It can't mean that he is completely innocent, can it? There must be something there, no matter how little," says Avieta, Rusanov's daughter (2: 313).

3

The Kostoglotov-Rusanov controversy has two culminations in the course of the story. Both take shape in an argument between the adversaries, and each concerns a profound subject matter.

The first argument arises in connection with Rusanov's reprimands to Yefrem Podduyev about the thoughts Lev Tolstoy's stories inspire in him: "What have you got against moral perfection?" snarled Kostoglotov. "Why does moral perfection give you such heartburn? Whom can it harm? Only a moral monstrosity!" And after hearing Rusanov's "The moral perfection of Lev Tolstoy and company was spelled out once and for all by Lenin and by Comrade Stalin and by Gorky!" "No one on this earth ever says anything *once and for all*," snaps Kostoglotov. "Because life would then come to a stop. And all the succeeding generations would have nothing to say" (2: 156–157).

Taken aback, Rusanov immediately comes to the usual conclusion that he should not refute an opponent but should check up on his political loyalties.

He is further convinced of the necessity of this by the second argument, in which the "holy of holies" in Rusanov's domain of forms— the dogma of "social origins"—is attacked by Kostoglotov:

> "That's a lot of nonsense—all that about social origin!" spat out Kostoglotov with disgust.... "They have stuffed your head with it."
>
> "What do you mean 'stuffed'? Will you answer for what you are saying?" exclaimed Rusanov shrilly, suddenly recovering his strength.
>
> . . .
>
> "We are not robots!" said Vadim shaking his head. "We do not take anything on faith...."
>
> "Well, how did you swallow all this stuff about social origin then? That's not Marxism, it's racism."
>
> "That's wha-at?" Rusanov almost roared with pain.
>
> "Exactly wha-at you heard," Kostoglotov flung back at him.
>
> "Listen to this! Listen!" Rusanov screamed, staggering and waving his arms for the whole room, the entire ward to gather around. "I ask for witnesses! I ask for witnesses! This is ideological sabotage." (2: 449–450)

The number of participants in this last argument grows. Vadim opposes Kostoglotov but not so convincingly; Shulubin supports Kostoglotov.

We read in the novel, "... all his youthful thrust, all the fiery impatience that was Vadim, all his great need to release his energies like a shot, to release himself and then give of himself," contradicted "the faded, watery moral ... about humility and love for your neighbor." He also could not accept lightly the attack on the concept of class character on which he had been raised. Although a stranger to schematics, he was sensitive to truth and falsehood.

Shulubin's introduction into the controversy robs it somewhat of its drawing room quality as it moves into the realm of major sociological and philosophical problems and conclusions. One cannot avoid noticing the special function of this character with respect to the structure of the novel as a whole. It is also impossible not to evaluate its unique artistic fullness and strength. There is an impressive account of Shulubin—an old Bolshevik is disillusioned with his beliefs and finds others. He is persecuted and rejected by everybody yet preserves an enthusiastic mind and spirit in the face of imminent death.

The chapter called "Idols of the Marketplace" is a conversation between Shulubin and Kostoglotov (actually it is only the former's monologue). It is a powerful denial reminiscent of Ivan Karamazov's "revolt." With words that could have been uttered by millions, Shulubin speaks of the "mortal fear" under which he had lived. For a quarter of a century he "cringed and kept silent" ("first I kept silent for my wife's sake, then for my children's, then for the sake of my own sinful self"). He speaks about the people who cannot actually believe in the lie that had been thrust upon them and about socialism deformed by the propaganda of hatred. ("You cannot build socialism on a surplus of material goods, because people may behave like buffaloes and trample the goods to the ground. Nor can you have socialism that never wearies of instilling hatred, because communal life cannot be built on hatred") (2: 488).

A socialism built on the negation of hatred, "an ethical socialism" (not capitalism, which "has been forever rejected by history anyway") has become Shulubin's new faith. "One should not direct people *toward happiness* because this is also an idol of the marketplace, 'happiness' is! One should direct them toward mutual affection. The beast gnawing at his prey can be happy, but only people can feel affection for each other! . . . That's what ethical socialism means" (2: 491).

Shulubin brings to the novel the critical theme of guilt, the responsibility to yourself and to history for the silence of fear and for the inability to say "No!" to crime, which amounts to treachery. This theme is uttered cryptographically in Bulgakov's novel *The Master and Margarita*.

"And when history," he concludes one of his accusations, "asks each of us at the grave, 'What was he?' there remains only one answer—Pushkin's: 'In our vile time . . . man is, whatever his element, either a tyrant, a traitor, or a prisoner! . . .' And if I remember that I've never gone to jail, and if I know for sure that I have never been a tyrant, that can only mean . . ." (2: 481–482).

This feeling of guilt does not leave Shulubin. Just after an exhausting operation, as Kostoglotov bends over his bed, Shulubin weakly yet repeatedly mentions the "fragment of the universal spirit" which he sees within himself and which he has preserved as a justification.

Kostoglotov makes no direct comment on ethical socialism, but the reader is left in no doubt about his opinion of the matter. He, like Shulubin, rejects hatred as the basis for any system whatsoever; thus they are akin in asking the ever disturbing and undecided question, "What do men live by?"

Common to both Kostoglotov and Shulubin is a rejection of the acquisitive drive, the craving for material things. "If we had enough white bread to crush under our heels and enough milk to choke us, we still wouldn't be the least happy. But sharing things we don't have enough of, we will be happy today," says Shulubin (2: 491). In the case of Kostoglotov the theme is extended to a distinctive Rousseauism. "What?" he exclaims as he sees a buyer in a store choosing a shirt, "... this fastidious little guy remembers not only the size of his shirt but the size of his collar as well. What is the reason for this refined sort of life? . . . If you remember the size of your collar, you're bound to forget something else, something more important" (2: 551).

Two new disinterested persons appear in the novel—the exiled Kadmins, elderly friends of Kostoglotov from the settlement of Ush Terek. Both of them are extremely happy that they are finally together. They are happy with their work, and their quiet life in their tumbled-down mudhut. They spend their evenings around a homemade round table with a rare ten-strand kerosene lamp on a tall stand.

Kostoglotov envisions a return to this life ("the wise man is satisfied with very little"). The chapter entitled "Memories of Beauty" contains lyrical descriptions of the impoverished life and colorings of the steppes and a lyrical conclusion affirming the modesty of his desires:

> He must not trust the tremors, the Beethoven chords. They are all iridescent soap bubbles. He must control his heart and believe nothing, expect nothing from the future, nothing better!
>
> Be happy with what you've got!
> Eternally—yes, eternally! . . . (2: 309)[3]

What a great contrast all this is with the materialistic Rusanovs—Kapitolina Matveyevna "with two silver fox furs around her shoulders"; Rusanov himself, who talks for hours to the speechless Federau "about his bathroom, the kind of tile that was installed on the floor and walls, about the ceramic bases and the soapstand . . . ," and so on.

Toward the end of the novel, the Kostoglotov-Rusanov axis is offered to the reader in its polarity—like a balance of weights. On one scale are Kostoglotov and Shulubin with their castigation of hatred and cannibalism, Yefrem Podduyev with his belated reflections on love toward people, the meek Kadmins, and the hundreds of unhappy patients on hospital beds—those who are doomed and those who have been fortunate enough to be saved from death by righteous doctors like Dontsova, who sees her own hard work as the only possible calling in life. In a word, on one side of the scale is a piece of folk life.

And on the other—is it not a little bit lighter on the other scale?

It is not light because Rusanov is not only the most vivid character in the novel, but the most significant one.

The vividness of Rusanov as a literary image lies in an almost physical awareness, on the part of the reader, of his sententiousness, his self-satisfied limits, and his callous performance of servile activities, because he is convinced of the infallibility of his master. The significance (the deeper meaning) is in the complete predictability and typicalness of his occupational features—the features of a torturer "isolated and mysterious," who ensnarls human lives in a web, "the web of forms."

The image becomes creatively transformed into a large and lifelike phenomenon. "Rusanov is a powerful embodiment of the dead idol of Stalinism," said Venjamin Kaverin at a discussion of the novel by the Moscow Writers' Organization (6: 160).

Is the idol really dead?

Lydia Chukovsky, in her article called "The Responsibility of the Writer and the Irresponsibility of the *Literaturnaja Gazeta*," writes in reference to S. Smirnov's verses, which eulogize Stalin:

"The reader must imagine for himself the climate in which *The First Circle* and *Cancer Ward* have attempted to appear on the scene. . . . Upon waking in the morning and in bed at night, we must remember that the great 'Requiem' by Akhmatova, the great lament for all those tormented and killed, has not yet been printed to this day but that these wretched lines by Smirnov, this lament at the grave of their torturer was freely published in the journal *Moscow,* 1967, No. 10'' (6: 126).

"The Rusanovs are not yesterday's danger. They were not the danger of 1955 alone,'' stated U. Karyakin at this same discussion in Moscow. "They are alive today, and they are dreaming that their day will come'' (6: 173).

Those who were "dreaming that their day will come'' evidently proved to be the most influential dreamers, insofar as Solzhenitsyn's novel has not yet seen the light of day in his own country. It is also noteworthy that the majority of the commentaries, whether they disapprove or partially approve, have dealt specifically with the character of Rusanov. ("Rusanov is unnecessarily one-sided and simple.'' "A weak character.'' "The character is publicistically overdone.'')[4]

In the text of the novel, Aviette Rusanov, "the diamond of the family,'' tells her father about Moscow. "Of course, there is a drop in the moral standards. A completely unknown Yevtushenko comes from nowhere, no rhyme or reason, bellows something, and waves his arms—he's long and lanky—and the girls go wild . . .'' (2: 317).

Seven years later Yevtushenko wrote these lines. Does their utterance not essentially imply that which the Rusanovs, who were "dreaming that their day will come,'' would not really want to approve of?

Kuda ešče tjanetsja provod iz groba togo!
Net,—Stalin ne sdalsja.
Sčitaet on smert'
            popravimost'ju.
My vynesli iz mavzoleja ego.
No kak iz naslednikov Stalina
            Stalina vynesti?![5]

(Where else from that coffin does the line lead! No, Stalin has not given up. He thinks he can outwit death. We carried him out of the mausoleum but how do we carry Stalin out of Stalin's heirs!)

4

"*Cancer Ward* has a depth equal to that of *The Death of Ivan Ilyich,*'' said the Soviet writer and critic, A. Borshchagovsky. A comparison of depth is not a comparison of artistic worth. However, we have already encountered attempts to find the stylistic influence of Lev Tolstoy in Solzhenitsyn's works. The examples used most often deal with analogous situations. The general theme of confrontation with death in the above two works draws them together in this way, for example:

Ivan Ilyich:
But Caius was really mortal, and it was right for him to die. But for me, Ivan Ilyich, with all my thoughts and feelings; for me it's a different matter. And it cannot be that I ought to die. That would be too terrible.

Rusanov:
... since men are mortal, he too would have to turn over his matters at some time or other. *At some time or other* but not just now! It's not frightening to die some time or other; it is frightening to die right now. Because, what will it be like? And what about afterwards? What will it be like without me? (2: 218)

Obviously the similarities are accidental and the closeness is not really organic. The conveyors of these utterances show too great a contrast. Unlike Ivan Ilyich, who confesses before the face of death, Rusanov is deeply convinced of the correctness of his way of life. In general, since comparative discoveries of similarities are often quite conditional (actually, is not the reverse more important for the scholar—how a given artist is not like any other?), then it is particularly difficult to find parallels with respect to Solzhenitsyn's style—because it is so indisputably original.

That peculiarly direct and suggestive narrative manner, drawn from oral *počvennost'* (discussed in the chapter "Resurrection of the Word"), is most easily traced in *Cancer Ward* by the theme of Yefrem Podduyev. Here are several lines concerning him, where not only the phraseology but the rhythm and the entire *sklad* of language seem to shed a light on the very object of communication.

Smolodu slyšal Efrem, da i znal pro sebja i pro tovariščej, čto oni, molodye, rosli umnej svoix starikov. Stariki i do goroda za ves' vek ne doezžali, bojalis', a Efrem v trinadcat' let uže skakal, iz nagana streljal, a k pjatidesjati vsju stranu kak babu, pereščupal.... (2: 115)

(From his youth Yefrem had heard, and even knew it was right about himself and his friends, that young people were growing up smarter than the old folks did. In all their days, the old timers had never made it to town; they were afraid, while Yefrem at thirteen was already riding horses and firing pistols. By the time he was fifty he had pawed the whole country as if it were a woman.)

Note how Yefrem's enthusiasm for Tostoy's story is related. ''No segodnja emu byla nexot' smertnaja otkryvat' rot, a priudobilsja on čitat' etu tixuju, spokojnuju knigu'' (2: 117) (But today a deathly reluctance to open his mouth had come over him, and he settled down to read this calm quiet book). His situation:

> Ne xotelos' Efremu ni xodit', ni govorit'. Kak budto čto v nego vošlo i povernulo tam. I gde ran'še byli glaza—teper' glaz ne bylo. I gde ran'še rot prixodilsja—teper' ne stalo rta. (2: 118)

> (Yefrem neither wanted to to walk nor to talk. It was as if something had been stuck into him and twisted inside. Where his eyes had previously been, there were no eyes; where his mouth had previously fit, there was now no mouth.)

And here the author has succeeded in finding the ''weighted-word,'' precisely in tune with the very pace of the disease.

> Streljalo emu ot šei v golovu, streljalo ne perestavaja, da kak-to rovno stalo bit', na četyre udara. I četyre udara vtalkivali emu: —Umer. —Efrem. —Podduev. —Tocka. —Umer. —Efrem. —Podduev. —Tocka. (2: 233)

> (Pain was shooting up from his neck right into his head, ceaselessly. Yet it had somehow begun to throb evenly in four-beat time. And the four beats hammered at him: Dead—Yefrem—Podduyev—Stop—Dead —Yefrem—Podduyev—Stop.)

As has already been indicated, what we have before us is not a stylization of the spoken features of an individual character but the joining of author with character in the interests of folk conversational speech elements. The same freedom and confidentiality, the same spoken, narrative phraseology is preserved in the novel independently of the thematic object of communication.

The differentiation in speech patterns among characters in the novel is significantly richer than in *The First Circle*. The language of Yefrem

Podduyev, of Chaly, of Asya, of Dyomka, or Shulubin, of the Rusanov couple is suggestively personal. Rusanov's style, for example, is typically didactic. Here is his lecture to Podduyev, who has been annoying him with his despondency.

> "The comrade has given you a good lesson, Comrade Podduyev. You shouldn't give in to sickness like that, and you shouldn't give in to the first priest-ridden booklet that comes your way. You are in effect *playing into the hands of. . . .*" He wanted to to say "of the enemy." In everyday life there was always some enemy to point to, but here on the hospital beds, who was their enemy?[6] (2: 229)

In conclusion—concerning the imagery and the lyricism in the novel: Actually, there is a great opportunity in this area for the investigator—picturesque words, lyrical words, simultaneously lyrical and picturesque, words that communicate a romantic theme, a character, or a landscape. Here is an example from Kostoglotov's interior monologue (at the beginning of the last chapter): "He could think of her now with neither greed nor frenzy. But it would be a joy to lie down at her feet, like a dog, like a miserable, beaten dog. To lie on the floor and breathe on her feet like a dog. He could not think of a greater happiness." This refers to Vera Gangart.

And her lips, the leitmotif of her diffuse portrait: "She had such responsive, light lips—like little wings" (2: 81). "They were somewhat lively and detached lips with their own individual purpose, not only to kiss"[7] (2: 82).

The character of Asya is romantic despite some naturalistic touches. It also uses a repeating picturesque detail—the "tuft" or "plume" of blonde hair. There is something of Pasternak's "abstract" drawing in its exposition. "She turned toward him, leaned forward without stretching out either arm; it was as if she were stretching both of them across the ruins of all the walls in the world . . . (2: 151).

The nature descriptions in the novel are lyrically personified by the experiences that move the hero or character. For example, Chapter 25 ("Vega") opens with Vera Gangart returning home on a sunny evening that smells of spring. Then there is the description of the night on the Ush-Terek steppes ("Memories of Beauty")—Oleg Kostoglotov's first night away from prison.

... The hard ground in the yard was white in the moonlight. He walked back and forth across the yard like a man possessed.... It was far from silent in the warm air of the early southern spring. It was like being at a huge rambling railroad station where the locomotives call and answer one another all night. From dusk to dawn camels and donkeys in their stables and yards bellowed like trumpets, greedily and festively throughout the town—about their conjugal passion and their confidence in the continuation of life. And this marital roar merged with that which roared in the breast of Oleg himself. (2: 295)

And (the concluding and perhaps most disturbing part of the novel) as if inscribed into the landscape of a spring morning, Kostoglotov walks out of the cancer ward and into a future he has not expected to find. "He had not expected to live to see this spring sun. And although there was no one around to rejoice at Oleg's return to life, no one even knew about it. But the sun knew, and Oleg smiled at it..." (2: 545).

Similarly lyrical and significant is the episode in which Kostoglotov buys flowers for Vera Gangart on his way to a meeting which never takes place.

And now he saw some flowers. The flowers were being sold to someone for some reason. He frowned. A vague recollection began to swim up in his mind, like a drowned corpse from a pool of murky water. That's right! That's right! In the distant, imaginary world of his youth, it had been the custom to give women flowers!

"These.... What are they?" he asked the flowerseller shyly.

"They're violets. What do you mean?" she was insulted. "One ruble a bunch." (2: 564–565)

6

"The First Knot":
August 1914

... since that time the composition of our nation has changed; faces have changed and a camera lens can never again find those trusting beards, those friendly eyes, those unhurried, unselfish expressions.

—*August 1914*

1

The fact that the novel *August 1914* is only the "first knot,"[1] thus only a part of the work that the author considers "the main project of his life," naturally hampers any discussion of it. Much that is unclear now will probably be clarified in subsequent parts; that which is only outlined will be completed.

Upon publication of the novel, many critical responses immediately appeared in which Solzhenitsyn's project was compared to Lev Tolstoy's *War and Peace*.

The conditionality and often the simple absurdity of these kinds of comparisons, and the fortuitousness of the similarities uncovered by them, have been discussed above. Comparisons by contrast, however, can at times actually help the reading of a novel.

The attentive reader immediately notices that in fact there is hardly any peace in Solzhenitsyn's novel. The relationship of peace to war (determined by a page count) in the first volume of Tolstoy's great epic novel is 1 to 1; in the third volume where the description of military events is the central interest, 1 to 2. Only sixteen of the sixty-four chapters in Solzhenitsyn's *August 1914* deal with other than military events in East Prussia (1–9, 42, and 57–62), which is a relationship of 1 to 4. But in contrast to Tolstoy's novel, these sixteen chapters are not structurally included in the fabric of the basic story. While the characters the reader meets on the very first pages of *War and Peace* reappear afterward alternately in military and in family situations, the characters in Solzhenitsyn's peace chapters seem to be parenthetic to the central, military description. This is what happens with the Tomchak family and several other personalities, apparently based on Solzhenitsyn's family background; thus, for example, the character of Sanya Lazhenitsyn is presumably the author's father (who, as Solzhenitsyn stressed in his autobiography, "volunteered for service in 1914, . . . became an artillery officer on the German front and was on active duty during the entire war . . ."). At the beginning of the novel Sanya Lazhenitsyn buys a newspaper and reads about Gumbinnen's victory, which is discussed much later in the novel. We again observe Sanya in Chapter 42, on the eve of his voluntary entry into the army. But then he completely disappears from our sight (until we perhaps meet him in the next "knot").

Other characters in the first seventy-five pages of the novel are also external with respect to the war theme. At the beginning of Chapter 61 we read: "For several weeks Ilya Isakovich had been warned by his engineer friends from Kharko, . . ." etc.; it takes some work for us to remember who this Ilya Isakovich is. The artistic purpose of this image (as well as that of Varsonofiev, the Stargazer from Chapter 42) is evident, but also evident is that in the composition of the novel it has a secondary nature.

Even the manner of narration in "the first knot" is original, distinguished not only from Tolstoy's but from that which we were accustomed to in Solzhenitsyn's last two masterpieces.

The manner is monological. This means that while the characters in *The First Circle* or *Cancer Ward,* whether or not they appear alone, are brought together in conflicts and episodes and reveal themselves through opinions and actions, the characters in *August 1914* are often related by the author and reach the reader only in the author's words. Of course dialogue is used, but the voice of the narrator—an informer and judge at times—quite often overwhelms the other voices.

His even, unhurried, methodical exposition accompanies this manner of narration. Somewhat fatigued by this, the reader may shut the book and then reopen it, as he looks for movement and closer contact with the characters whom the author has granted independent action.

There are two such main characters in the novel: Samsonov and Vorotyntsev. Accordingly, there are two plot lines—the larger is Vorotyntsev's, the smaller, inner one is Samsonov's.

The larger or main plot is the following: Colonel Vorotyntsev of the General Staff is sent by headquarters to General Samsonov, who is in command of the Second Army. He goes through the active front, where he associates with various commanders and soldiers. He participates in battles himself, experiences the destruction of an army, and with a small group of men he breaks through the surrounding forces and comes to his own. As a result of what he has seen, he is convinced of the inability of the high command to direct the movement of the greater masses of soldiers. The stupidity, the ignorance of military matters, and most of all, the self-seeking dishonesty of the high-ranking officers, who are subordinates to the Supreme Commander but protected by the court behind his back, have brought Samsonov's army to ruin. Twenty thousand were killed and seventy thousand taken prisoner.

Upon his return Vorotyntsev reported all this to the Grand Duke. The scene is last in the novel and thus ends the plot line.

Vorotyntsev is intelligent, generous, and courageous. During his interpretation and evaluation of events (entrusted to him by the author), a number of commanding officers pass before the reader: Colonel Krymov, General Nechvolodov, Colonel Pervushin, and others—all masters of corps, divisions, and regiments. Negative characteristics are frequent. There is General Blagoveshchensky, who feels himself a "Tolstoyan Kutuzov" and has "never commanded one company during wartime—and suddenly here is a corps." General Kluyev has spent forty years in military service but never in that time has he taken part in a war; "Kluyev had the facial trimmings of a military man, especially his moustaches, a mark of decorum in an officer. But on closer inspection his face was not a military one, in fact there was no face at all—it had no real distinctive features" (252).

It is neither criticism nor exposure that makes the figure of Vorotyntsev so vivid in the novel's structure;[2] rather, it is his enthusiastic attention to the main figure in a war—the soldier. "The people in the war" thanks to this become a kind of third main character and in unison with the other two achieve the expression of those traits in the national spirit that one must understand in order to pursue any history. The traits of self-sacrifice, courage, and indifference toward death are examples.

The Dorogobuzh regiment under the command of Colonel Kabanov had to cover the retreat of Kluyev's corps. "In the fourteenth year of the twentieth century the only weapon left to the Dorogobuzh regiment to use against the German artillery was the Russian bayonet. Evidently the regiment was doomed to perish. . . ." The regiment, which had lost its commander, detained the enemy; and in "every company fewer than one in twenty survived."

"And this miracle," we read further,

> was due to more than just the fortitude of the officers. Half the troops were reservists, who a mere month ago had come to the induction center in bast shoes, fresh from their villages, their fields, their plans, their families. On the contrary, they understood nothing, knew nothing of European politics, the war, the battle their army was fighting, or the objectives of their corps whose number they did not even know. Yet they did not run away, they did not dodge or waver, but by some unknown power they crossed the barrier, on the one side of which is love of self and family and the need for self-preservation—but across it you do not belong to yourself any longer, only to cruel duty. They raised themselves three times and went into fire with noiseless bayonets. (354)

Another significant episode, which takes place toward the end of the structural plot line, is tied to this folk heroism. Vorotyntsev breaks through the enemy siege and overtakes a group of soldiers from the Dorogobuzh regiment. They are carrying the body of their deceased colonel on a stretcher in order to bury him in his native soil. ("Twenty-five miles! And carrying those stretchers! What faith, what strength was it that had sustained them!") And later when Colonel Kabanov's body has to be buried under a hillock among the pines, a funeral is improvised. Blagodaryov, Vorotyntsev's volunteer orderly, suddenly comes forward and proclaims to "the tall pine tops":

> "In peace let us pray to the Lord!"
> It was so compelling, so powerful, so exactly like a church service, that no further invitation to join in was needed. Olonetsky and Luntsov and two other men immediately understood and responded. They crossed themselves and bowed to the East, each from where he stood:
> "Lord have mercy on us!"
>   . . .
> "Having besought the grace of God, the Kingdom of Heaven, and the remission of sins for them and for ourselves, let us commend ourselves and one another and our whole life unto Christ our God."
> And higher than the sun, beyond the sky, directly to the throne of the

All-High, in one voice, fourteen men sent up the familiar hymn, not in
supplication but in sacrificial offering, in renunciation:
  "To Thee, O Lord. . . ." (450–451)

Among the military men met by Vorotyntsev are two striking
figures—his companion Arsenii Blagodaryov (Senka), gladly accom-
panying the colonel who had taken such a liking to him, and the battery
sergeant, Major Terentii Chernega, who "was such a picture of
strength." What makes these two characters especially memorable is
Solzhenitsyn's artistry in making the narrative "strange" by submerg-
ing it into the common parlance of the characters. Entire paragraphs that
describe life at the front or at a manor house occupied by Russian
troops, a rest before the new battle, are presented in the speech tonality
of Blagodaryov, a capable infantryman from a Tambov village, who
finds himself at the lakes in East Prussia.

  "And one of our batteries got a direct hit! Right between the guns!
Baroom! Baroom! And an ammunition box up in the air and—exploded
itself! exploded! Horses ran in every direction, and people covered with
soot crawled away—those who were still alive. Senka's mare got scared
and shied off the path. Senka could hardly get control of her—and all
the way into the forest" (242).

  Arsenii Blagodaryov and Chernega are associated with the most vivid
and visual scenes among the many battle episodes sprinkled through
chapters 15–55. For example, Blagodaryov and Vorotyntsev are bar-
raged by German artillery fire in the Vyborg regiment's trenches.
("This Vorotyntsev had never experienced in his life.") There is the
battle in which Chernega's battery engages in order to guarantee the
withdrawal of his and other Russian troops. The Russian army was
retreating in confusion. ("There is a bridge somewhere and we must
rush to this bridge, and if it is knocked down, we are lost.") This is the
battle in which Chernega's innate talent to command, which has been
dwindling away, is awakened in him.

  And Chernega roared at his men like a lion, drowning out all other
  commands, the grumbling, the neighing, and the clanging. The battery
  had known its sergeant-major, but they had not really known him, because until that night the war had not yet begun for them. That lion's roar

got it across to them that from now on they would have to strain every muscle, that if the horses refused, the men themselves would have to haul the guns. (382)

Placed here and there in the novel are "survey" chapters that do not contain characters. According to the author, they are necessary in order to further elucidate the flow of events. For the reader who values inner movement these chapters are a burden; the movement in the novel is sometimes slow even without them. The film sequences are probably included in the novel to stimulate movement. Several film images, symbolic with respect to the setting and to the human fates crowded upon it, are perhaps most interesting of all: the image of the burning windmill, for example. The arms begin to rotate slowly, thus forming a disintegrating wheel in the air (228), but another wheel had bounced off an ambulance cart in motion.

> and alone! passing by! rolling on ahead!
> The Wheel!! it's getting even bigger,
> It's even bigger!
> It's filling up the whole screen!
> *The Wheel!* It rolls on, lit by fire!
> —all alone!
> uncontrollable!
> crushing everything!
> *THE WHEEL!!!* (287)

In "the first knot" proverbs as "epigraphs in reverse" are used in an original way; they seem to make a clarifying summary at the end of certain chapters. The last chapter of the book ends with the proverb, "UNTRUTH DID NOT BEGIN WITH US; NOR WILL IT END WITH US." It is the end of Vorotyntsev's mission—his impassioned, accusatory report is turned down by Staff Headquarters.

2

Samsonov's plot has previously been called an inner one not only because it is smaller (Chapter 10, the Ostrolenko headquarters—

Chapter 48, death), but because of the special significance of the image that makes it central to the novel and carries it beyond the framework of the plot proper.

The epithet "calm" is the leitmotif of Cavalry General Samsonov's portrait and, perhaps, that of his entire spiritual aspect. Samsonov's calm face "was generally never distorted," "his smooth forehead remained calmly round, even, and unfurrowed," "his calm thick lips were shielded by his calm moustache and beard."

But it is precisely a calm concentration that Samsonov lacks because of the pressures of commanding an army. Not for a moment can he "be left alone to clear his thoughts." Furthermore, in this new kind of war the commander is in fact isolated from those whom he must direct and control.

His staff is put together ignorantly and "dishonestly," without his knowledge; the senselessness of the direction and haste of the march, reproachful telegrams and harassment from headquarters, and perhaps a premonition of catastrophe, all torment Samsonov. "Stirring in his mind were the invisible, inaccessible things that were taking place out there—in the sand, in the forest, within a seventy-five mile radius—things which 'his staff officers did not hurry to burst in and tell him about." A feeling that he had become "not an active force but just a representative of events" arose in him; ". . . a certain layer of his soul seemed to break away from some other layer, and it began little by little to slide slowly away. And Samsonov was constantly listening to this inaudible movement."

A series of episodes follows, reflecting the disintegration of the commanding general's spiritual world. They are written with a power rare for Russian literature of this century, and they are significant because beyond this disintegration is another breakup—that of an entire army; perhaps something even greater—the disintegration or displacement of the emotional and spiritual life of a whole nation.

Among these episodes is Samsonov's prayer (291–292). And his insomnia on the same night: "but near his ear, a clear voice with shades of prophecy seemed to breathe:

"Assu . . . assu. . . ."
"Assume command?" he asked hopefully.
"No, assume . . . ," denied the adamant voice.

"Am I asleep?" guessed his reclining spirit.

"No, thou shalt be assumed!" replied the angel relentlessly.

Ruin approaches. Crushed by the Germans, the Russian troops run away.

The culmination of this theme is: The commander rides up to two battalions made up of stopped runaways "to inspire them to perform a military miracle." With a voice "that had a certain affinity to the tolling of Russian church bells," he turns to them with a reproach. "A general's speech," writes Solzhenitsyn, "has the characteristic of an immediate call to action—it tolerates no retorts from listeners and does not expect any arguments" (364).

But Samsonov appears to hear the objections that several officers, standing before him in formation, might make (how they had come under a barrage "that the commander himself had probably never experienced; how only three Russian batteries had replied, and even these were short of ammunition"); and the soldiers ("It's your job to preach to us; but we're not stupid, we know what really happened").

And the ruin is completed.

Suddenly, as he spoke, "Samsonov's confidence came forth out of his instinct to command." He suddenly felt abandoned by everyone. It was with that side of his soul, which always strove to draw spiritual strength from the soldiers, that he discovered this loneliness.

Samsonov "slumped weakly in his saddle." Having just exhorted the two guilty battalions to advance forward, he orders retreat. "The greatest decision of his lifetime had been made in one moment. It was as if the north became south; the east, west; it was as if the sky above the pine trees had been turned upside down. When and how had Samsonov lost the battle? When and how—he had not noticed" (348).

Further: Samsonov's farewell to the confused retreating troops, his last meeting with Vorotyntsev (Chapter 44, the larger and smaller plot lines intersect here), and the concluding episode (429–430)—death.

Samsonov's character in "the first knot" has the utmost significance in modern Russian prose. In connection with this, it is impossible not to linger once again over the most important structural base in Solzhenitsyn's writing—his language.

The language of "the first knot" is undoubtedly new and a further perfection of that style inspired by the idiom of *počvennost'* with which Solzhenitsyn has entered the world of literature. There is here, perhaps more than in his other works, a harmony between the discovered word and its context, a phraseological-intonational system in which the word joins with the rhythm, sound, and stylistic coloring that totally surrounds this word.[3]

Here are two excerpts from Chapter 44. Samsonov and the remainder of his staff pass through such a countryside:

> The forest narrowed even more; it became a thin wedge. Until now only the pine tops were lit by sunlight, but here their road turned to the left, and the semi-gloom gave way to the full blaze of a bright crimson sun, which had just risen over the top of another line of trees—the endless thirteen-mile stretch of the Grunfliess Forest, thick and dark, waiting for the retreating Russian army. About four hundred and fifty yards before the edge of the forest, a ravine dropped off to a meadow around a river, full of quivering mist, rising upward into steam. (391)

And the commander-in-chief makes farewell rounds among the confused remains of battalions and regiments. The colorings and the inner rhythms at times resemble Rublev's icon painting.

> It was like a church holiday, but it was strange without the chiming of church bells and the gay kerchiefs of womenfolk. It was as if a crowd of sullen peasants from the nearby villages had gathered on a hillside and a landowner or a priest on horseback was slowly riding around them, promising either to give them land or paradise in the next life for their suffering in this.
>
>   . . .
>
> The army commander had a kind voice. All the men, as he passed them to bid farewell and thanks, followed him with looks of good-will. None of their glances were malicious. That bared head with an expression of exalted grief; that recognizeably Russian, purely Russian hairy face—a black thick beard, with plain large ears and nose; those powerful shoulders, weighed down by an invisible burden; that slow regal advance, reminiscent of the czars before Peter—all this could not be subjected to curses. (393–394)

It is necessary to comment on several chapters that are external to the military theme of the novel: Chapter 42, which deals with a meeting between Sanya Lazhenitsyn, his friend and Varsonofiev, "the Star-gazer," and chapters 57–62, where the significant conversation be-tween engineers Arkhangorodsky and Obodovsky and the younger gen-eration of radicals takes place.

The relation of these chapters to the succeeding "knots" in the work planned by Solzhenitsyn will be obvious. It would serve no purpose to try to determine its character now. With regard to relationships between events in the story of "the first knot," there is some resemblance to the relationship of the poetry section in Pasternak's *Doctor Zhivago* to the remaining prose section—it is partly its own message and partly a key.

Many motifs that have been encountered in the author's earlier works are contained in the opinions that Varsonofiev imparts to Kotya, "the Hegelian," and Sanya, "the Tolstoyan": Nerzhin's reflections about *narodničestvo* and the people ("Do the people have *responsibilities?* Or only *rights?*" "all these *narodniks* don't want to help anything less than an entire people right away; until then they refuse to save them-selves"); the dispute between Sologdin and Rubin on the dialectics of historical development ("The State does not like a break with the past. It specifically likes gradualness. A break or a leap is destructive for it"); thoughts about higher justice ("the spirit of which exists within us, before us and without us"); thoughts on the "harmony of the soul" ("We are only called upon to put our soul in perfect order"), and so on.

A turning to the realm of spirit is the basis for all these statements. This same inclination is contained in military sections of the novel. Beyond the surface presentation of military events, the author tunes in on the manifestations of the spirit of the personalities that interest him and the spirit of the greater mass of soldiers.

The crisis of this spirit is evidently the inner thesis of "the first knot." We read:

> In a four year war that had strained the popular spirit, who can take it upon himself to point out the decisive battle? They were countless, many were ignominious rather than glorious, gobbling up our strength and belief in ourselves, joylessly and uselessly taking away our bravest and strongest men, leaving a lesser breed. Nevertheless, it can be claimed that the FIRST Russian defeat defined and set the tone for the whole conduct of the war for Russia . . . from the very first time our spirit was stifled, and our former self-confidence was never regained. . . . (349)

Was this crisis of spirit not its regeneration? Or was something lost forever?

Take the significant lyricism of these sentences dedicated to the memory of the deceased in Samsonov's vanquished army: "The press lumped them all together as "GRAY HEROES," and felt that it had done what it could. But there were no photographs and it is a pity that since that time the composition of our nation has changed; faces have changed, and a camera lens can never again find those trusting beards, those friendly eyes, those unhurried, unselfish expressions" (355).

In a conversation between the two engineers and some young people (Chapter 62), Ilya Isakovich Arkhangorodsky makes a noteworthy objection to the young Naum Galperin's assertion that revolution is a form of progress: "a reasonable man cannot be for revolution, because revolution is a process of prolonged and insane destruction. Above all, no revolution ever strengthens a country, but only ravages it for a long time. And the bloodier, the more drawn out, and the more costly it is to a nation, the more likely the revolution will be called GREAT" (536).

This collision of opinions is artistically reflected in the main thread of the novel; the revolutionary lawyer Lieutenant Lenartovich whose leading principle in his relationship to war is "the worse it is, the better," deserts his platoon and unexpectedly encounters General Samsonov making his farewell rounds. This scene is impressive for its portrayal of a combat of spirits.

> As he [Samsonov] approached, Lieutenant Lenartovich did not hurry to move aside. He could not tear his eyes, his happy eyes, from this spectacle! Ah-ah-ah that's what you need! Then you'll immediately become so kind. Ah-ah-ah, that's when you'll soften up, you with all your medals, when you get a good crack over the head! Just you wait, just wait—there's more coming.
>
> As he stared thus, spellbound with hatred, the army commander rode straight up to him. And as if directing the question at him personally, although he did not address him by rank, he gazed into the lieutenant's eyes with a bovine, resigned, vacant look and asked paternally, "And you there?"
>
> What a mistake! And there was no time to think, he could not get away. Everyone was waiting to hear what he would say. But what? Should he lie? That was no good either.... Then, the best thing was to blurt out something quickly.

"Twenty-ninth Chernigov regiment, your excellency!" And at the same time, instead of saluting, he made a vague movement with his hand like the wave of a fish's fin. (One day that would be something to tell Veronica and his Petersburg friends, if he ever survived!)

. . .

"My special thanks to you men of the Chernigov regiment. . . ." And he nodded a dismissive, understanding, grateful nod. He slowly rode on. His horse also seemed to nod, as it lowered its head deeply.

The Commander-in-Chief's broad back made him appear more than ever like a fairy tale hero, downcast and sad, before the signpost at the parting of the ways: "If thou goest to the right. . . if thou goest to the left. . . ." (403–404)

The critical theme of *August 1914* will probably sound louder in succeeding "knots," which will also bring the narrative closer to our times. This theme is set off from several Tolstoyan motifs.

"In this case we might appear to find consolation in Tolstoy's conviction that it is not generals who lead armies, nor captains who lead ships and companies, nor presidents and leaders who run governments and political parties. But the twentieth century has shown us too many times that it is precisely *they* who do such things" (350).

7
Significant Realism

He could no longer take things naively and dispassionately. No matter what he saw in life from now on, a gray specter and a subterranean rumbling would arise within him.

—*Cancer Ward*

Life is symbolic because it is significant.

—B. Pasternak, *Doctor Zhivago*

1

Solzhenitsyn's so-called prose poems are rarely mentioned in the many reviews of his work that have appeared in the West. Meanwhile, these miniatures, which occupy perhaps a dozen pages, are rare and distinct sources for discerning the author's image as well as important inner features of his artistic manner.

One of the contemporary Soviet writers who uses the prose poem form extensively (perhaps better called a sketch) is M. Prishvin—"The Calendar of Nature," "Facelia," "Forest Thaw," and many others. Careful attention to detail, an intense gaze, and a suggestive and accurate image system are common to both writers. But there are essential differences.

Let us compare. Take, for example, Prishvin's sketch "Goose in the Sun": "The sun returned. The goose dipped its long neck into the pail, scooped up some water for itself with its beak, splashed itself a little, scratched something there under each feather, and set its tail wriggling in a lively spring-like motion. When it had washed and cleaned everything thoroughly, it raised its silver shining wet beak upward towards the sun and began to cackle."[1]

The author admires the slice of life, glittering before him. The scene is beautifully completed by the sudden break—it "began to cackle." But in Solzhenitsyn there would almost certainly be an extended design of associations, perhaps lyrical but all the same it would be abstract, because it would lead the reader toward the eternal "what" and "how" of life. It might sound through the words; it might only be conjectured about.

"The Duckling" is one of the most memorable of Solzhenitsyn's miniatures. Its theme is similar to Prishvin's. A duckling has been hatched by a chicken. Here it is, alone and helpless, on the palm of the author's hand.

> What keeps it alive? It weighs nothing at all. Its little black eyes are like beads; its feet are like those of a sparrow. Give it a tiny squeeze and it would be no more.
>
> Yet it is so warm with life. Its little beak is pale pink like a manicured nail and slightly splayed. Its feet are already webbed. There is yellow in its plumage, and its downy wings are just starting to protrude. Its personality has already set it apart from its brothers.

This could be the end but Solzhenitsyn goes on:

> And soon we will be flying to Venus. Now, if we cooperatively set out to do so, we could plough up the whole world in ten minutes.
>
> But never! Never, with all our atomic strength, could we manufacture in a test tube, even if we were given the feathers and bones, never could we assemble such a fragile, pitiful, little yellow duckling. . . . (5: 224–225)

The motifs in the prose poems are heterogeneous: places in Russia, beloved or just visited by the author ("Lake Segden," "A Journey along the Oka," "The Ashes of a Poet"); things he has accidentally seen along the way ("The Bonfire and the Ants," "The Elm Log," "The Small Ball"); thoughts ("Reflections," "We Will Never Die"), and so on. All of these, however, are bound to a single inner theme—the earth is good and life is priceless; but people do not appreciate or else distort both.

"I stand under an apple tree in bloom, and I breathe. Not only the apple tree but the grass around it give off moisture after a rain. There is no name for the sweet fragrance that fills my lungs. . . . This is perhaps that freedom, that single most precious freedom that prison takes away from us—the freedom to breathe freely as I do now. No food on earth, no wine, not even a woman's kiss is sweeter to me than this air steeped in flowering moisture and freshness'' (''Freedom to Breathe'').

A night spent in the mountains in tents—the thunder, the din, and the alternation of darkness and lightning—elicits that radiant feeling of being at one with the primal world of creation: ''we forgot to be afraid of the lightning and the downpour and the thunder—just like a droplet of water in the ocean, which has no fear of a hurricane. We became an insignificant and grateful part of this world...'' (''A Storm in the Mountains'').

Life is more beautiful the closer it is to the plenitude and authenticity of nature. The rejection ''of the most hideous creature in the world, on six fast rubbery paws with dead glass eyes and a bony, vacant mug...''[2] instead of a living four-legged animal is reminiscent of Yesenin's train image in ''Prayers for the Dead.''

> Čert by vzjal tebja, skvernyj gost'!
> Naša pesnja s toboj ne sživetsja.
> Žal', čto v detstve tebja ne prišlos'
> Utopit', kak vedro v kolodce. . . .

> (The devil take you, you nasty guest! Our song is not used to you. It's a pity that in your childhood you did not drown, like a bucket in a well. . . .)

Yesenin is close to Solzhenitsyn in the *počvennost'* of his poetics. (''Since the time of Koltzov, the Russian earth did not produce anything more native, natural, appropriate, and generic than Sergey Yesenin,'' wrote Boris Pasternak.) Nerzhin values a volume of Yesenin's poetry at the *sharashka*. Kostoglotov reads some lines from the poem ''Soviet Russia'' to Zoya.

The miniature ''In Yesenin Country'' is also hardly accidental. The nature of poetic talent, as it uncovers the beauty of the earth and in turn conceives of this same beauty, is well presented.

> ... I come out onto the steep banks of the Oka and stare into the distance with amazement. Was it really that far-off deep strip of the Khvorostov Wood which evoked the enigmatic line: ''The pine forest, clamorous with the wood grouse's lament. . . .'' Is this the same Oka,

meandering through the meadows: "Haystacks of sun in the water's depth . . .'"? What a bolt of talent the Creator must have hurled into that cottage to the heart of that quarrelsome boy, for the shock of it to have made him find so much beauty—near the stove, in the pigsty, on the threshing floor, in the fields; beauty which for a thousand years others had simply trampled on and not noticed!

The theme of the criminal desecration of beauty, the ruin and defacement of monasteries and churches also reverberates. "The Ashes of a Poet"[3] and the prose poem, "A Journey along the Oka" with its lyrical description and tone both deal with this. Here is an excerpt from the latter:

> Traveling along country roads in central Russia, you begin to see why the Russian countryside has such a soothing effect.
> It is because of its churches. They rise over a ridge, or a knoll toward the hillside, descending down to wide rivers like red and white princesses, towering above the thatched and wooden roofs of daily life with their slender, carved and fretted belfries. From far away they nod to each other; from distant, separated villages they rise toward one sky.

Here is the tolling of the eventide bell that rolls over the earth, reminding man "that he must abandon his trivial earthly cares and give up one hour of his thoughts to life eternal."

And the bitter contrast of the ending:

> Our ancestors put their best into these stones and these belfries—all their understanding of life.
> Come on, Vitka, buck up and stop feeling sorry for yourself!
> The film starts at six, and the dance is at eight. . . ."

Certain elements in these prose poems evidently demand a deeper reading.

For example, "The City on the Neva" praises the architectural and plastic beauty of Peter's capital ("What luck! It is not permissible to build anything here anymore—you can't squeeze a wedding cake skyscraper onto Nevsky Prospect, you can't slap together a five-story box on the Griboyedov Canal").

In the end, after noting all the forgotten curses and bones upon which all this had been erected, there is the question: "It is terrible to conceive that our disastrous, chaotic lives, our bursts of protest, the groans of men being shot by firing squads, and the tears of our women—will also be forgotten. Can all this too give rise to such perfect, everlasting beauty?"

How can this be taken? "The groans of men being shot by firing squads and the tears of our women" in the Stalinist years of trouble were not associated with any kind of creativity or necessity. There was brutality and evil, which would be unacceptable to any court of justice.

Akhmatova immediately comes to mind:

Eto bylo, kogda ulybalsja
Tol'ko mertvyj, spokojstviju rad.
I nenužnym priveskom boltalsja
Vozle tjurem svoix Leningrad.

. . .

Zvezdy smerti stojali nad nami,
I bezvinnaja korčilas' Rus'
Pod krovavymi sapogami
I pod sinami černyx marus'.[4]

(It was a time when only the dead smiled, happy in their tranquility. And Leningrad dangled like a useless pendant around its prisons. . . . The stars of death stood over us, and innocent Russia writhed under the crunch of bloodstained boots and under the wheels of Black Marias.)

The question is no doubt rhetorical. It is terrible to think that *it would ever be possible to forget this!*

The prose poem "Lake Segden" is a jewel. The beginning is:

No one ever writes about this lake and it is not talked about very much either. All roads to it are barred, as though to an enchanted castle, and over each road hangs a forbidding sign—a simple sign.

Be it man or wild beast who notices this sign in his path—turn back. Some earthly power has put that sign there. It means: past this point it is forbidden to ride, fly, walk, or crawl.

Near the road policemen with pistols often sit in ambush.

Does this lake have a specific geographical location? How are we to understand this? If it is real, then why does it have a fairy-tale aura about it? The wild beast and bird hearken to a mute sign that has been placed there not by some local sheriff but by some "earthly power." Then there is the enchanted forest ("The people have been frightened away. No one goes into this forest anymore"); there is the beauty of the lake; the mysterious lyrical isolation from the world ("If there is a world beyond the forest, it is unknown, invisible...").

And further:

> ... A cruel prince, a cross-eyed villain, has captured the lake; there is his summer cottage, there is his bathhouse. His evil brood goes fishing here, shoots duck from his boat. First a wisp of blue smoke over the lake, then in a moment—the shot.
> There beyond the forest the surrounding province stoops and heaves. While here all the roads are closed so that no one interferes with them.

Is this not merely a sketch of local color in a framework of almost seditious self-criticism related in an unusual way?

The last lines appear to restrain such an interpretation:

> Beloved, deserted lake.
> My native land....

How then should we read this? As a symbol? The poetic world of Solzhenitsyn is not a world of symbols. His artistic tools are realistic.

But his reality is often a special kind—a significant reality. This must be explored more thoroughly.

2

At an interview with a journalist Lev Tolstoy declared this paradox: "It is harmful and bad," he said, "when a work of art is published during the lifetime of its author; for when he writes he is not free. He will most certainly be thinking of *what* they will say about his work, how it will be received, etc., etc."[5]

Tolstoy's idea loses whatever paradoxical quality it has when it comes up against the compulsory self-censorship situation in which Soviet writers work. The effect of this self-scrutiny has its own artistic coefficient (unfortunately, often disregarded by the critics): first, the choice of motifs, conflicts, and images that emerge as a result of such fears as "what will they say?" "how will it be received?" "will they publish it?"; second, that which cannot be articulated by a writer who is constrained by the lack of freedom.

As a result this self-scrutiny may take the form of what we generally call cryptography, a cryptography not in the sense of codifying a text, a method used by Pushkin in the tenth chapter of *Eugene Onegin,* but one that circumvents the obstacles of censorship—a cryptography consisting of literary devices that embody themes in such a way that it is not immediately apparent but requires a second reading.

This second reading can be offered in the form of a hint (allusion) or another form in the nature of allegory, fable, or symbol, but with more clarity of purpose with regard to the expression of the author's dissenting "I."

In both cases, the second reading is based on parallel associations, ideas, and interpretations that arise in the reader.

Just like censorship itself, cryptography has its place in Russian literature.

Makogonenko, the author of the book *From Fonvizin to Pushkin,* brings out an example of cryptographic allusion which he discovered in Knyazhnin's tragedy *Olga*. This tragedy, reported to be a free translation of Voltaire's *Merope* and adapted for Russian life by the "imitative Knyazhnin," deals with the theme of succession to the throne. Its main characters are Princess Olga and Svyatoslav, whose mother surrenders her power and refuses to remain on the Russian throne. "What is the throne to me? It's not for me to possess but for my son. Perish, cruel mother. That heart of a barbarian! That soul, thirsting for power, which relishes her son's sad hour—all to spend the days of her life in pompous pretense, she accepts for herself his inheritance."

Catherine acted differently toward Pavel, who was already fifteen years old when Knyazhnin wrote his tragedy. In Makogonenko's opinion the situation presented in the tragedy is meant specifically as an allusion to and perhaps is the reason for the empress's ensuing animosity toward the dramatist. "This was," writes Makogonenko, "a recommendation to Catherine. The exaggerated praise of a mother who did not allow herself even to think of taking power from her son, who summoned death upon herself for the mere possibility of assuming the throne, was more than just daring in the Russia of that time. Russian tragedy did not yet know about such allusions."[6]

In February 1835 Pushkin notes in his diary: "Censorship did not permit the following lines in my tale about the golden cockerel—"

Carstvuj, leža na boku
(Reign, as you lie on your side)
and
Skazka lož', da v nej namek,
Dobrym molodcam urok. . . .
(The fable is false but in it a hint, a lesson to good lads. . . .)

In the works of postrevolutionary writers and poets, control over verbal creation was far more effective than the censorship of czarist times. We can refer to Yesenin, who so keenly foresaw the tragedy of the Russian countryside:

Slyšite l'? Slyšite zvonkij stuk
Eto grabli zari po puščam.
Veslami otrublennyx ruk
Vy grebetes' v stranu grjaduščego.

(Do you hear? Do you hear the ringing rap? It is the rake of sunrise in a virgin wood. With oars of cut-off arms you row out to the land of the future.)

There is also an allusion in his dramatic poem "A Land of Scoundrels." The hero says to Zamarashkin, "who sympathizes with the Communists":

Vse vy nosite oveč'i škury,
I mjasnik paset na vas noži.
Vse vy stado!
Stado! Stado!
Neuželi ty ne vidiš'? Ne pojmeš'?
Čto takogo ravenstva ne nado?
Vaše ravenstvo—obman i lož'.
Staraja gnusavaja šarmanka
Etot mir idejnyx del i slov.
Dlja glupcov—xorošaja primanka,
Podlecam—porjadočnyj ulov.

(All of you wear sheep's clothing, and the butcher prepares his knife for you. All of you are a herd! A herd! A herd! Can it be that you don't see? Don't you understand? That such equality is not needed? Your equality is a fraud and a lie. This world of lofty deeds and words is an old twangy street-organ. A perfect lure for fools, a proper trap for scoundrels.)

As we turn to contemporary works, we find elements of a second reading (or double meaning) in Yevgeny Yevtushenko, a poet of Communist beliefs but of a more liberal understanding of artistic freedom than his party leaders. In his cycle of poems called "From an American Notebook" (Znamya No. 1, 1968), Americans speak about America, but their statements occasionally acquire two different local meanings; among the native voices we hear the author speaking about himself and his country.

> Uxodit uverennost'...
> Pomnitsja, kljalsja ja strašnoj božboju
> o stenu bašku prolomit'
> ili—stenu—baškoju.
> Baška pocarapana, pravda,
> no, v obščem, cela.
> A čto so stenoj?
> Uxmyljaetsja svoloč'—stena,
> Kto-to na nej ravnodušno menjaet reklamy,
> portrety...
> Uverennost', gde ty?

(Confidence is leaving me... I remember how I swore a sacred oath to break my skull against the wall or the wall with my skull. True, my skull is scratched a bit, but in all, it's in one piece. And what about the wall? It's smirking, that bitch of a wall. Someone is indifferently changing the ads on it, the portraits ... Confidence, where are you?

Similarly, "Monologue of a Broadway Actress" and especially "Monologue of a Polar Fox on an Alaskan Fur Farm," where we read such lines, for example:

> Kto v kletke začat, tot po kletke plačet,
> I s užasom ja ponjal, čto ljublju
> Tu kletku, gde menja za setku prjačut,
> I zverofermu—rodinu moju....

(If you're hatched in a cage, you'll weep for the cage; I understood with horror that I love that cage, where they hide me behind a screen, and the fur farm—my native land.)

Allusion may be recognized also in certain critical works. An example is Arkady Belinkov's book[7] on the works of Tynyanov. The author's "unruly" thoughts are camouflaged by the context, which holds them within the framework of an evaluation of Griboyedov's times while inwardly addressing them to our own times. Here are some excerpts.

"The age of Nicholas was especially igonimious in that hunger was not called hunger but a magnificent success reached only through the zeal of the authorities; slavery was not called slavery but a higher freedom; the stifling of the human mind was beneficial censorship. . . ."

And this statement, in which there is without a doubt a reference to Stalin's times:

It is necessary to discredit by every means possible the confidence of those who do not care a pin about anything but their own power, who see democracy not as an end but as a means. Disguised in this affirmation is a repulsive complacent confidence in the belief that some realize and others do not realize this goal, and that some should lead toward this goal and all the rest, whether they are dedicated or not, must follow these leaders. But the time will come when it will suddenly be discovered that the leader himself does not know anything except that the faith which he is able to inspire—through cruelty, cunning, and deceit—is only useful to himself and to a dozen of his slaves. Since this faith was inspiring (in various ways) over a ten-year period, then many thousands of slaves will, of course, never forgive the fact that having overthrown the idol—with whom they jointly committed their crimes—their own souls were spat upon. . . .[8]

Various forms of double reading are present in Yuri Olesha's *Envy* (with its double interpretation of the Kavalerov–Andrei Babichev antithesis); also in Pasternak's *Doctor Zhivago* (with its apology for the human spirit and the right of creative independence for the artist); and especially in Bulgakov's novel *The Master and Margarita,* where the cryptographical condemnation of terror, cowardice, and treachery is brought forth with a remarkable strength and courage for that time.[9]

In "post-thaw" poetry there is considerable allegory in Bella Akhmadulina's "The Fable of the Rain," where the rain (Pasternak-

like) is the symbol of poetic talent and inspiration threatened by the
"drought" of a censorship terror.

The New Year ballad "Wings" by the Ukrainian poet Ivan Drach, is
interesting for the significant, humorous treatment of its theme—that
there are certain circumstances in which a person's talent is a burden or
even a danger. It is humorous by virtue of its purely literary associations
with Pushkin's famous "Why the devil did I have to be born in Russia
with a soul and talent?" The plot of the ballad is this. Out of the many
presents that the New Year brought the good people, Uncle Kirill was
left with a really unusual one—wings. They grew out of his back to the
great surprise and fright of himself and his dear ones.

> A woman cried: "All people are just people,
> To each his own, according to fate:
> To one powders, if he catches a cold,
> To another felt boots,
>   to another sour cream in cabbage soup,
> But to my viper, God forgive me—
>   wings on his back!"

> Thus Kirill lived and grieved,
> And then in order to recover his freedom
> He would sharpen his ax on a stone,
> Put his wings on a log and chop them off....

> But the owls scream
> Ashamed to the stars of Kirill's earthliness.
> Popping through his nightshirt during the night,
> His wings would rise up again in the morning.

> Thus Kirill lived with his ax
> He did well even with his wings.
> He covered his yard with a roof of wings,
> And fenced himself in with his wings.
> Feather by feather poets took them away
> In hope that their muse would take wing
> Aesthetes composed prayers to them
> But the desecrated wings only dreamed of the sky....

> To one—a new hen,
>   To another—a barrel of meanness,
> To one—the sun in his palm,
>   To another—a fig as big as a potato,

To one—fuzz on his beard,
  but to Uncle Kirill—what an unlucky man!
  —Wings![10]

3

  The above examples of allusion and cryptographical allegory do not really have direct counterparts in Solzhenitsyn's artistic mode. What is comparable, however, is the significance (that is, the special depth of meaningfulness) of images, which gives rise to parallel associations and ideas within the reader. This extends and deepens the reading.

  There is one place in *Cancer Ward* that beautifully reveals the artistic nature of this significance. In the next to the last chapter of the novel, one of the episodes described is Oleg Kostoglotov's visit to the local zoo.

  The spiral-horned goat is the first animal he stops in front of. The goat "had stood there a long time just like a piece of sculpture, like a part of the rock itself. And when there was no breeze to make its straggly hair flutter, it was impossible to prove that it was alive, that it was not just a trick." This sight generates the idea of steadfastness, a firmness of will so necessary to life, in Oleg. "Here is the kind of character one needs to endure life," he decides with admiration.

  Now, in front of the next cage, the squirrel's, he is seized by a contrasting idea—the futility of daily life. It "was for some reason in a wheel, although no one had forced it to go there or enticed it with food. It was attracted only by the illusion of sham activity and movement. . . . The squirrel's reddish, spindly body and grayish-red tail unfurled in an arc of mad racing. The cross pieces of the wheeled staircase rippled until they were completely fused together. All of its strength was being used up. Its heart was about to burst!"

  The next few lines suggest to us to what extent the image suddenly has become a symbol for Kostoglotov. "There was no external force in the cage that could have stopped the wheel or rescued the squirrel from it. There was no power of reason which could have made it understand: 'Stop! It's all in vain!' There was only one inevitable way out—the squirrel's death."[11]

  And the conclusion is given a significant interpretation: "Here were two meaningful examples—on the right and on the left of the entrance—two equally possible ways of existence with which the zoo greeted young and old alike'' (2: 556–557).

The origin and character of Kostoglotov's deepening associations at the zoo can be presented visually in two columns—*"he sees"* and *"he interprets."*

A sign before a cage reads: "White owls do not thrive in captivity."

So they know that! And they still lock them up! What kind of degenerate owls did thrive in captivity.

"The porcupine leads a nocturnal life."

We know what that means: they summon it at half past nine in the evening and let it go at four in the morning.

"The badger lives in deep, complex burrows."

Aha—just like us! Good for you, badger, how else can one live? He's got a snout of striped ticking, a real convict.

A black [bear] with a white "tie" was standing and poking its nose into the wiring between the bars. Suddenly it jumped up and hung by its front paws from the grill.

It wasn't so much a white tie but a kind of priest's chain with a cross over its chest. It jumped up and hung there. How else could it show despair?

In the next one was a tormented grizzly. It kept stamping the ground restlessly, longing to walk up and down its cell, but there was only room for it to turn around, because the length from wall to wall was no more than three times its own.

So according to a bear's measuring scale, it was not a room but an isolation cell. (2: 558)

All these associations together form an entirely new, completely abstract, and thus even greater depth. "The most confusing thing about the imprisoned animals was that, supposing he took their side and had the power, Oleg could not even begin to break their cages open and free them. This was because *they had lost the idea of rational freedom when they lost their home surroundings*. Their sudden freedom might have a terrible effect on them.[12]

The sad, hairless, as if shaven, monkeys remind Kostoglotov of many of his friends sitting in prison somewhere even to this day. Then he is stunned by a notice on another cage: "The little monkey that used to live here was blinded because of the senseless cruelty of a visitor. An evil man threw tobacco into the Macaque Rhesus monkey's eyes."

"But why? Just like that! It's senseless! Why?... He was not described as an agent of American imperialism. All it said was that he was evil..." (2: 560).

"From this comparison it is clear that the evil man hurling tobacco into its eyes is definitely meant to be Stalin," Solzhenitsyn stated later at a meeting of the Secretariat of the Soviet Writers' Union in Moscow on 22 September 1967 (6: 54).

The idea of Stalin and his crimes is recalled again with the tiger image: "... in his whiskers, yes, the expression of his rapacious nature was concentrated in his whiskers. But his eyes were yellow... Oleg's thoughts became jumbled, and he stood looking at the tiger with hatred. An old political prisoner who had once been in exile in Turukhansk, had met Oleg in the camps and had told him that those eyes were not velvet black but yellow" (2: 561).

The zoo episode ends with a paragraph that could be called "a revelation of devices," but it is above all important as the author's declaration of his special deepening awareness, vision, and interpretation of life: "His [Kostoglotov's] brain was so twisted that he could no longer take things naively and dispassionately. No matter what he saw in life from now on, a gray spectre and a suberranean rumbling would arise in him" (2: 559).

An examination of examples of significance in Solzhenitsyn's works could fill dozens of pages. Therefore, we will limit ourselves to only a general group and several illustrations.

There are many significant details. Let us take the description of Ivan Denisovich during a meal. He "could not allow himself to eat with his hat on." With a spoon he had cast from aluminum wire, he checked "what he got in his bowl." He sucked out the brittle fish skeleton but did not eat the fish eyes—"when they were boiled out of their sockets they floated in the bowl separately—big fish eyes." At the same meal a significant observation seems to be mentioned in passing. "There behind the table, before dipping his spoon in, a young fellow crossed himself. That means he's a West Ukrainian and a new arrival too. As for the Russians, they've forgotten which hand to cross themselves with" (1: 14). Also significant are the quilted jacket, the cause of the narrator's first burst of anger at Matryona ("she had dirtied the sleeves on the frozen mud around the timber"); the book of Yesenin's verse "in a paper cover depicting a shower of autumn leaves"—Nerzhin gives it to Spiridon; the round (unquestionably round) table at the Kadmin's mudhut, and many, many others.

The entire story "The Right Hand" is built on details, on the attention and reflections with which the author, and the reader after him, regards the hand of an unhappy, ailing patient, a former Chekist—a hand "so small it is incapable of pulling a certificate out of his wallet," yet at one time it had struck down men on foot "from a horse, with a sweeping backhand stroke."

The character types are significant. Matryona, in whom the author divines features of the righteousness in the folk spirit; Rusanov, "the embodiment of the dead idol of Stalinism" according to Kaverin; General Samsonov, "a lamb of seven poods," whose features—both inner and outer—are telling and meaningful. Episodic characters are also significant—the old railroad car inspector, Kordubailo, for example, in "An Incident at Kretchetovka Station." An incident occurs at the station: hungry "returnees"[13] attack a trainload of flour which is being transported in open wagons. A sentry shoots one of them in the head, and a conversation regarding this is taking place at the station commandant's office. Kordubailo's remarks are entirely "of the soil," and his own "against the current" interpretation of what happened is noteworthy.

> "What else could he do?" Valya argued, tapping her little pencil, "you know he was on duty. You know he's a sentry."
> "Well, that's right," nodded the old man, dropping large pieces of red makhorka ash on the floor and on the lid of his lantern. "That's right. . . . Everyone wants to eat."
> "What do you mean?" the girl frowned. "Who is this everyone?"
> "I mean you and I, for instance," Kordubailo sighed.
>
> . . .
>
> ". . . Where was the flour going? To the Germans?"

"Well, that's right," the old man did not argue a bit. "But those boys weren't Germans either. They're our people too."

. . .

"And why did they slice the sacks open?" said Valya indignantly. "What type of people would do that? Our people?"

"The sacks must have been sewn up," said Kordubailo, wiping his nose.

"All that flour poured out of sacks and being wasted, Comrade Lieutenant. How many children could have been fed?"

"Well that's right," said the old man. "But in such a rain the rest of it will get wet in the open wagons." (1: 146–148)

The narrative pictures, varied in thematic extent and purpose, of ordinary and psychological situations, nature descriptions, and conflicts are significant too. It is difficult, for example, to read *The First Circle* and not feel the intensity of the scene between Nadya and Shchagov ("Leaning her forehead against the middle pane, Nadya touched the other cold panes with outstretched hands. She stood like someone crucified on the black cross beams of the window"), not to discern the turning toward Eternity in Kondrashev-Ivanov's picture "The Castle of the Holy Grail," not to catch that which is said behind Yakonov's simple words at the church ruins: ". . . Yet he stood there with his elbows leaning against dead stones and he did not want to live any longer."

From Pasternak's *Doctor Zhivago: "Life is symbolic because it is significant."*

But to repeat: Symbolism is not the spirit of Solzhenitsyn's prose. It is realistic in its own direct and rigorous ties with a real environment. Perhaps Solzhenitsyn's realism needs a more precise epithet.

This has occurred many times with the definition of the term realism. There was naive realism, which appeared in the stories of the seventeenth century and in *Poor Liza;* the realism of *Anton Goremyka* ("natural'naja skola"); the sentimental-critical realism of *Poor Folk;* just simply critical realism, which extended through all of Russian literature of the nineteenth century and was suppressed at the beginning of the thirties in this century; romantic realism—from Turgenev to Alexander Grin, also Gorky to his revolutionary phase and the early

Gladkov and Fadeyev of Soviet literature; the psychological realism of Lev Tolstoy; the psychoanalytic and religious-philosophical realism of Dostoevsky; the poetic realism of "The Lady with the Dog" and "The Bishop"; the symbolic realism of *Doctor Zhivago;* finally, socialist realism, which arose from the negation of a critical examination of life and from the disregard for sincerity as genuine to inspiration, thus making it incapable of establishing any kind of artistic genuineness.

The realism of Alexander Solzhenitsyn is a *significant* realism.

Notes

Chapter 1

1. Pushkin's "Prophet" is a poem that emphasizes the writer's mission to enlighten the people: "Arise o Prophet, see and hear/Be filled with my will/Go forth over the land and sea/ And set the hearts of men on fire with your *Word*."

2. Per Egil Hegge, *Svenska Dagbladet*, 28:6, 1971.

3. Translated from Alexander Solzhenitsyn, *Collection of Works in Six Volumes* (Frankfort/Main: Posev, 1970), 6: 53. Further translations from this collection will be referred to simply by volume number and page number.

4. Volume 1, M (1958), pp. 12–13.

5. Almanac, House of Art, 1, PTB, 1921.

6. *Novyj Mir,* No. 1 (1967): 231. Compare Boris Pasternak, *Prose 1951– 1958* (University of Michigan Press, 1961), 2: 43–44.

7. Roman Goul, "Reading *August 1914,*" *New Journal,* 104 (1971), 191.

8. In 1950 the author of this sketch published an article exposing such "disguises." The article, "Overseers," appeared in the weekly *Posev* and was reprinted later in New York's *Novoe Russkoe Slovo* (New Russian Word).

9. *Literaturnaja Rossija,* 25 Jan. 1963; and *Sovetskaja Kirgizija,* 30 Jan. 1963.

10. See, for example, p. 261 of the second volume of *Gulag Archipelago* (YMCA Press), where the autobiographical element is confirmed by the author.

11. "Bless you, prison," says Solzhenitsyn himself in *Gulag Archipelago,* v.2.

12. Dostoevsky's term for a kind of democratic Slavophilism. *Počva* = soil; figuratively, the people. Therefore *počvenničestvo* is a return to the people.

13. N. Åke Nilsson, "Hos Boris Pasternak," *Bonniers Litterära Magasin* (Stockholm, 1958), p. 621.

14. Boris Pasternak, *Doctor Zhivago* (Ann Arbor: University of Michigan Press, 1958), p. 9. Further translations from this work will be referred to simply by title and page number.

Chapter 2

1. "How rare the fortunate times, when you can feel as you want and say what you feel" (Tacitus). The numbers in parenthesis refer to the pages in the Russian edition: K. Marx and F. Engels, *Sočinenija,* vol. 1 (Moscow, 1955).

2. N. Gumilev, "The Word."

3. A more detailed account of this can be found in my work dealing with the Russian literary language in the postrevolutionary epoch: *Language and Totalitarianism* (Munich: The Institute for the Study of the USSR, 1951).

4. Pushkin, *A Journey from Moscow to Petersburg.*

5. *Skaz*—an oral narrative manner in which features of the narrator in a particular social milieu are portrayed.

6. From a private correspondence with the author of this book (3 Nov. 1952).

7. This is discussed in the following chapter.

8. A term used by V. Shklovsky, *ostranenie* literally means "making strange" (from *strannyj*—strange"). The presentation of reality is creatively transformed.

9. Alexander Solzhenitsyn, *August 1914* (Paris: YMCA Press, 1971), p. 239. Further references will contain only the page number.

Chapter 3

1. *Novyj Mir,* no. 1 (1964). See also A. Solzhenitsyn, *Sobranie Sočinenij,* 6: 243.

2. For more details see my article "The Image of the Narrator in Solzhenitsyn's Story *One Day in the Life of Ivan Denisovich,"* L. Rzhevsky, *The Language of Creative Writing* (New York University Press, 1970). Also, in *Studies in Slavic Linguistics and Poetics in Honor of Boris O. Unbegaun* (New York-London, 1968).

3. Italics are mine. L. R.

4. If we use B. A.Uspensky's term "nositel' avtorskoj ocenki.'' See B. A. Uspensky, "Poetika Kompozicii," in *Struktura Xudožestvennogo teksta i tipologija kompozicionnoj formy* (Moscow: "Iskusstvo" 1970), pp. 20–21.

5. This portrayal of the bricklaying activity is artistically and ethically the best example of the construction theme in postrevolutionary literature. Of course one must look rather for the nature of its inspiration—in Dostoevsky's notes on prison labor in *House of the Dead*—since one can hardly attribute enthusiasm for socialist construction to the zeks of the Stalinist camps.

6. Georg Lukacs, *Solzhenitsyn* (London: Merlin Press, 1970), p. 24.

7. *Oktjabr,* no. 4 (1963).

Chapter 4

1. *Sharashka* comes from the word *šarašit'*—"to work foolishly." The expression *šaraškina kontora* indicates a place where shabby work is done.

2. Some foreign critics are inclined to see in the novel traces of the "influence" of Dante, aside from the obviously analogous title. See V. Gre-

benschikov, "Les Cercles Infernaux Chez Soljenitsyne et Dante," *Revue Canadienne de Slavistes* 13 (1971): 2–3.

3. For example, Nerzhin—nine, Volodin—eight, Stalin—four, etc.

4. *DO*č' *T*rudovogo *NAR*oda—"daughter of the working people."

5. *DI*tja *N*ovoj *ER*y—"child of the new era."

6. The name *Zhvakun* comes from the Russian word for ruminants or cud-chewing animals—*žvačnye*.

7. Note also the name of a convicted activist, a party spokesman who always carries a dictionary of English idioms with him ("you have to know the enemy")—Satanovich (4: 433–434).

8. The italics are mine—L. R.

9. Potemkin, a statesman and favorite in Catherine II's court, so wanted to impress his empress on her tour of an area that he built a sham village. Thus the method referred to is a pretense for prosperity.

10. In *Cancer Ward* there is just such a reference. Oleg Kostoglotov is standing in front of a tiger's cage and is reminded of Stalin ("In his whiskers, yes, the expression of his rapacious nature was concentrated in his whiskers. But his eyes were yellow!" And: "An old political prisoner, who had once been in exile in Turukhansk and had met Oleg in the camps, told him that those eyes were not velvet black but yellow") (2: 561). In 1913 Stalin was exiled in Turukhansk.

11. About these sources, see the valuable article by Edward J. Brown: "Solzhenitsyn's Cast of Characters," *Slavic and East European Journal* 15, no. 2 (Summer, 1971): 162–165.

12. "Realism chiseled down to symbol"—as said by Nemirovich-Danchenko.

13. *Narodničestvo*—in the second half of the nineteenth century a movement in Russia for the cultural and political development of the peasant (*narod*—"folk").

14. We find a similar thought in some lines by a Hungarian poet, Petyofi:

We walk about bowed to the ground.
We hide away, fearing the stranger's gaze.

15. This building belongs to the KGB.

Chapter 5

1. OSO (*Os*obyj *O*tdel) A special department that acts in place of a court.

2. In Russian: "A zabolel u Efrema—jazyk, povorotlivyj, ladnyj, nezamet-

nyj, v glaza nikogda ne vidnyj i takoj poleznyj v žizni jazyk. Za polsta let mnogo on etim jazykom poupražnjalsja. . . .''

3. In the YMCA Press edition (Paris 1968) the chapter ends differently:

Be happy with what you've got.
Eternally—yes, eternally! . . . There I will live without you.
Oh! Don't tease me, breath of spring!

The explanation for the difference in the texts is nowhere to be found. One can only suppose that the author himself shortened the text of the Paris edition and discarded, for example, the last phrase—the beginning of Werther's aria (Massenet) with ''do not tease'' substituted for ''do not arouse.''

4. A somewhat similar situation from the past comes to mind. When Ostrovsky wrote *It's a Family Affair—We'll Settle it Ourselves* in 1849, M. P. Pogodin with the help of personal contacts managed to avoid censorship difficulties and had the play published in *Moskvitjanin*. But the offended Moscow merchants protested the performance of the play. The committee considered their complaints and found Ostrovsky guilty of not balancing his negative characters with some heroic characters worthy of imitation: ''with due respect to our merchants in whom the qualities of fear of God, goodness of soul, and uprightness of mind constitute their typical and permanent characteristics.'' The czar's resolution: ''It was printed for no good reason, its staging is prohibited.'' The comedy remained, however, in libraries and bookstores.

5. Y. Yevtushenko, ''Heirs of Stalin,'' 1962.

6. The italics are mine—L. R.

7. In the edition published by the YMCA Press, this fragment reads as follows: ''They were somewhat lively and detached lips which seemed to flutter from her face like a lark into the sky. All lips are made for kissing, as were these, yet these had a special purpose—to murmur about something bright'' (68).

Chapter 6

1. Solzhenitsyn designated his book as *Pervyj uzel* (''first knot'') in the Russian edition.

2. Criticism is traditional in Russian literature. L. Tolstoy said in the *Sevastopol Stories,* for example, that a general is most often ''an obsolete creature, weary, spent, as he endures patiently and unconsciously the right amount of humiliation, inactivity, and extortion for the achievement of his rank. They are people without sense, education, or energy'' (Jubilee ed., 4: 293).

3. This harmony has not been felt by several commentators, who have complained about the experimental word choice in the novel. However, wrenching

obscure or unusual words from a text does not constitute an analysis of the language of an artistic work, and the criterion itself of "obscurity" or "unusualness" is debatable. "Unusual" words, like the creative language chosen by the artist, often carry within themselves "something" *beyond* their direct meanings in a particular context. We call this the language of *art*. "The light from the artistic hiding places falls upon the word in different ways," wrote Sergey Klychkov, the poet and narrator of folk tales. He was destroyed by the Stalin terror. "And everything depends on how the word connects up with another word, how it takes the other word by the hand in order to enter into a smooth and majestic verbal round dance. People say every girl is beautiful in a round dance" (S. Klychkov, "Lysaja Gora," *Krasnaja Nov'*, No. 5 (1923).

Chapter 7

1. M. Prishvin, *Sobranie Sočinenij v Šest' Tomax* (Moscow, 1956), 3: 426–427.

2. "Sposob dvigat'sja." See *Grani,* No. 80, p. 9.

3. By Polonsky; see the first chapter in this book.

4. Anna Akhmatova, "Requiem," The Fellowship of Foreign Writers (Publishers) 1960, p. 8.

5. *Novyj Mir,* No. 3, 1963.

6. G. Makogonenko, *Ot Fonvizina do Puskina* (Moscow, 1969), p. 268.

7. A. Belinkov, *Yury Tynyanov,* 2nd ed. (Moscow, 1965).

8. *Ibid.* pp. 359–360. For a more detailed discussion on cryptography see L. Rzhevsky, "Tajnopisnoe v russkoj posleoktjabr' skoj literature," *Novyj Žurnal,* No. 98 (1970). David Frolich, *Cryptography in Soviet Literature* (Ph.D. dissertation, New York University).

9. See L. Rzhevsky, "Pilatov grex" (on cryptography in Bulgakov's *The Master and Margarita*) in *The Language of Creative Writing*. It also appears in English in *Canadian Slavonic Papers,* Vol. XIII, I, 1971.

10. Translated from my Russian version of the Ukrainian. In the Russian collection of poems by Drach, *Protuberancy serdca,* "Wings" was omitted.—L. R.

11. In *Gulag Archipelago* (1:69–70 in the English edition) Solzhenitsyn seems to give a realistic extension of this image of a squirrel in a wheel. He tells about a conference not far from Moscow, where at one point the name of Stalin was being applauded for ten minutes. Everyone was getting completely exhausted but no one could be the first to stop applauding. The one who finally decided "to jump from the revolving wheel" was subsequently arrested.

12. The italics are mine—L. R.

13. These were prisoners who had surrendered to the Germans during a hopeless battle. Soviet forces then recaptured them and sent them to detention camps in Russia.

Index

Creator and Heroic Deed
was composed in VIP Times Roman by
The Composing Room, Grand Rapids, Michigan,
printed by Thomson-Shore, Inc., Dexter, Michigan,
and bound by John H. Dekker and Sons, Grand Rapids, Michigan.
Project Editor: James R. Travis
Book design: Anna F. Jacobs
Production: Paul R. Kennedy

Solzhenitsyn: Creator and Heroic Deed

Leonid D. Rzhevsky

translated by Sonja Miller

The seven essays in this volume examine Solzhenitsyn's "inner themes" coming into conflict with Soviet ideological censorship, and his skill in the creative realization of these themes through an approach that introduces innovations both of structure and, pronouncedly, of language and style.

Taken together, the essays serve as an excellent introduction to Solzhenitsyn's writings. While they contain considerable biographic detail, the major emphasis is on the characteristics of Solzhenitsyn's style and usage. Highly useful to the Solzhenitsyn scholar, the book's lucid style also makes its substance extremely attractive to the general reader.

The original Russian publication (in West Germany in 1972) received high praise in both Europe and America: "This book helps to better understand the writer and his work and its special significance for the Russian of today" (*Slavic and East European Studies,* Canada, vol. 17, 1972); "The critical research of L. Rzhevsky is among the best not only in Russian, but in all the world literature on Solzhenitsyn" (*The New Russian World,* New York, January 14, 1973); "Rzhevsky—together with the reader—attentively and lovingly run through the best works of Solzhenitsyn" (*Russian Thought,* Paris, February 8, 1973).

Leonid D. Rzhevsky is Professor Emeritus of Slavic Literature at New York University and was formerly a lecturer at the Lenin Institute, Moscow (1941), and Lund University, Sweden (1953–1963).